Stirling
—— AND ——
The Trossachs
CHARLES McKEAN

THIS is the first time that Stirling
and the Trossachs have been treated to
an illustrated architectural guide such as
this. It reveals the splendours of our
heritage and draws our attention to places
that perhaps we take for granted. We
have been shown the way by these
architects of the past. Let us hope that
we can meet the challenge of the future
with equal skill and excitement.

The support given by
Stirling District Council
for this publication
is greatly appreciated.

ARCHIE FERGUSON
President
Stirling Society of Architects

Published by

The Royal Incorporation of
Architects in Scotland

and

Scottish Academic Press
33 Montgomery Street
Edinburgh

ISBN 0 7073 0462 8
An RIAS/Landmark Guide

Sterling from the Abby-Cragg.

National Galleries

Stirling and its District straddles the great divide
between the Highlands and the Lowlands of
Scotland, encompassing bits of both, but
consisting principally of large tracts of historic
no-man's land includes the southern part of what
used to be the county of Perthshire and the
northern part of what used to be Stirlingshire,
ranging from the coalfields of Fallin in the east,
the railway frontier town of Crianlarich in the
north, and the great mass of Ben Lomond in the
west, to Glaswegian commuter belt of the
Strathblane valley in the south. Dominating the
district is the Carse of Forth which cuts an
immense swathe between the Highland hills to
the north and the Lowland hills to the south
getting flatter and wider as it travels east only to
be blocked, physically and psychologically, at its
eastern end by the crags of Stirling, Abbey Craig
and Dumyat. Until well into modern history, the
Carse was largely impassable from south to
north save by tracks known only to natives
through the treacherous moss which in places
could be up to 12 feet deep. Merchants,
travellers, politicians and armies were compelled
to seek the only main road, paved in parts, and
the only bridge. In order to do so, they had to
go right through the town of Stirling for the
moss and marshes washed the very base of its
rock.

That simple topographical fact explains why so
many of the significant battles in Scottish history
were fought near to Stirling: the battle of
Stirling Bridge (1297) in which William Wallace
defeated the English; the battle of Bannockburn

Stirling from the north in 1672,
drawn by Captain John Slezer
(courtesy, National Galleries of
Scotland).

Opposite: Aerial view of Stirling
looking west along the Carse of
Forth (RCAHMS).

Stirling from Torwood, 1672 by Slezer. This would have been the view of the town seen by Gilbert Blackhall in 1637: clearly demonstrating why the only route from the south of Scotland to the north lay through the gates of Stirling itself.

SIR DAVID LINDSAY, in his 1530 satire *the Testament and complaynt of our sovaerane lordis papyngo* uses the form of the dying statement of the king's pet parrot to satirise the abuses of the church, in part of which he apostrophises Snawdoun (the ancient name for Stirling):

Adew, fair Snawdoun! With thy
   touris hie,
Thy Chapell Royall, park, and tabyll
   rounde!
May, June and July walde I dwell in
   thee,
War I ane man, to heir the birdies
   sounde
Quhilk doith agane thy royall roche
   redounde.

(1314) whose Scottish victory re-established the independent Scottish nation; the squalid battle of Sauchieburn (1488), in which King James III was defeated by an army including his son, and murdered immediately thereafter; and the battle of Sheriffmuir (1715) which ended the first Jacobite Rebellion. In between times, the town and castle of Stirling were subject to a number of sieges, commotions and invasions, witnessing the murder of one Regent, the suspected poisoning of another, the murder of the leader of the Douglas faction, and — *inter-alia* — one of the finest flowerings of Scottish culture in the country's history. For during the 15th and 16th centuries, Stirling was the favoured seat of the Stuart Kings, and the architecture of the castle, and the poetic output of the time comprise some of Scotland's finest cultural heritage.

That period represented the peak of Stirling's royal ambitions. After the Union of Crowns in 1603, Royal visits to Stirling were rare and from the later 17th century onwards, the rock slumbered in a past that was already over 100 years old. In the early 19th century, there was a substantial development of pleasant classical streets and villas which in turn was engulfed by the enormous expansion of grand Victorian suburbia both in Stirling and in Bridge of Allan, following the introduction of the railways and the influx of wealthy merchant commuters from Glasgow.

Castle and Town

Sitting on a volcanic outcrop, controlling both the Carse of Stirling and the only major route from the south of Scotland to the north, Stirling lay at the heart of Scotland and Scotland's history. The town developed in the lee of the castle, down a shorter and steeper "tail" than its counterpart in Edinburgh. The first recorded royal use of the castle was the death there in 1124 of King Alexander I who is thought to have dedicated its original chapel. Until 1603 Kings of Scotland stayed there regularly and, during the 15th and 16th centuries, it became the centre for the Court, the historian Pitscottie recording that James III *tuik sic plesour to duall thair that he left all wther castellis and touns in Scotland, because he thocht it maist pleasentest duelling thair.*

Until the creation of new roads round the bottom of the rock, c. 1842, everybody travelling by road from the south of Scotland to the north had to go through Stirling itself. The most

dramatic record of that requirement has been left by Gilbert Blackhall, a priest of the Scottish Mission in France, illegally in Scotland in 1637, and in fear for his life, partly as a result of a vision which had warned him to beware of Stirling. He wrote: *if I go forward, I must pass through the town, for I see a long stone wall at every side of the town gates.* He met two gentlewomen at Torwood and *prayed them to show me how I could go to the bridge un-going through the town. They said we are sorry you have come so near the town for now you can go neither back again nor turn to any hand unremarked.* In the company of the two gentlewomen, Blackhall entered the Burroughs (or Barras) Yett (the main gate to the Burgh Muir) going uphill to a lodging. *The lodging pertained surely to some person of quality, for it was very fair, a great court builded on three quarters, and a baluster of iron on the side of the garden which had a fair and large parterre. By good fortune, there was nobody at all in the lodging . . . they did take me through an alley of the garden to a stair which bestanded by the side of the Town Wall. The stair was all of stone, and but little more than one foot broad and very deep down. The wall was on the left hand of it and nothing on the other side to save people falling from it. My horse made great difficulty to enter it but one of the gentlewomen did take the end of the bridle and I did go behind and push him down.* The mansion in question was either Moir

Above: Stirling from the King's Park in the 17th century, attributed to Vorstemans. The town wall is clearly apparent, as are the marshes at the bottom. On the left is the King's Knot with its formal gardens and trees.

5

of Leckie's or the Argyle Lodging, and Blackhall survived to tell the tale.

Subsequent visitors noted the intense narrowness and steepness of the street — at least as far up as the Market Place or Broad Street which, according to Alexander Campbell in 1802, had *every advantage of a free circulation of air and breadth of area. This being the principal street, and that leading directly to the castle, in former times the nobility had their dwelling houses in it. Baker's Wynd is the most populous of any of the lanes of Stirling. The other principal streets viz. St John Street, Mary's Wynd and Friar's Wynd are narrow and dirty habitations of idleness and poverty.* The *narrow and irregular* streets noted by Walter Scott projected so close to Queen Victoria's carriage in 1842 that, according to Sir Thomas Dick Lauder *her Majesty might have shaken hands with the well-dressed persons who were the temporary occupants of the windows of these mean old tenements.* Those buildings with projecting staircases were demolished in the name of civic improvement. After the mid-19th century the Upper Town became abandoned into a slum attracting progressive demolition from the end of the First World War.

Organisation of this Book
This book begins with a guide to what used to be called *the Rock*, the inner suburbs and the hinterland of Stirling to its immediate south and east. The remainder follows the convention of linear routes: to the north, north-west and north via Bridge of Allan, Dunblane, Callander, Balquhidder, Killin and Crianlarich; the western route through Blairdrummond, Thornhill and Aberfoyle to Inversnaid; and the south-western route through Gargunnock, Killearn, and Drymen, to Strathblane on the south and Loch Lomond on the west.

Not all buildings mentioned in the text are illustrated. The numbers adjacent to a building description are keyed in to the maps at the rear. Most building descriptions follow the order of home address, date, architect (if known), then description. Indices to architects and buildings may be found at the rear.

Right of Access
Many of the buildings described in this guide are either open to the public or are visible from the road. As many are privately owned and not open to the public, readers are requested to respect the occupiers' privacy.

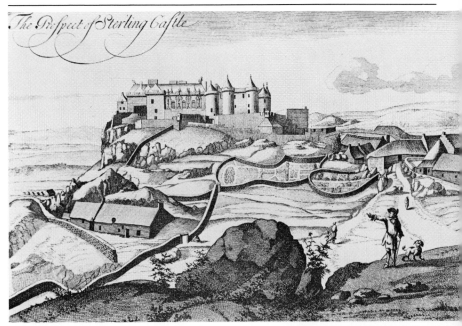

The Prospect of Sterling Castle

1 **Stirling Castle** 14th century onwards.
The entry is through an elaborate European-style
scheme of outer defences designed by Captain
Theodore Dury 1708-14, the masons being the
celebrated Thomas Bauchop of Alloa, and James
Watson. The **New Port,** controlled by the over-
port battery and the spur battery, leads to the
first Guardroom Square, controlled in its turn by
the Queen Anne battery, and then by the second
gateway of the over-port battery. The sentry
boxes, corbelled out from the angles are capped
with stone, ogival domes, similar to those at Fort
George and Edinburgh Castle.

The visitor is then faced by the **Forework:**
one of the most *castle-like* entries in Scotland.
Dating from about 1500, it consists of a long
wall protected by a ditch, terminated with two
quasi-towerhouses at either end — the Prince's
Tower to the west and the decapitated
Elphinstone Tower to the east. At the centre is
the towered gateway which, as can be seen from
the old engravings, originally consisted of four
three-storeyed towers with conically roofed
caphouses over corbelled parapets, not unlike
illustrations from 15th century French illustrated
manuscripts. The two centre towers containing
guardrooms survive, reduced by a storey and
decorated with a 19th century crenellated
parapet. They flank the **Gatehouse** whose main
entry is stone vaulted and protected by a

RCAHMS

Top: Stirling Castle and the
Tiltyard in 1672 drawn by John
Slezer. It shows the gateway with
its four towers still complete, and
the houses on the right which were
removed for the Esplanade in the
early 19th century.
Above: the Forework as it is now.

portcullis — as are the foot passages on either side. The gatehouse debouches into Lower Square. **The Grand Battery,** to the north, is built above late 17th century kitchens which served the Great Hall. *The Commissary told us,* wrote John Ray in 1692, *that the greatest inconvenience . . . in case of seige was that, upon the discharging of the great guns, the water in the wells would sink and the wells would become dry.* The oldest surviving building is the **Mint,** probably 14th century, beneath which a long vaulted passage leads into the Nether Bailey, and — originally — to an entrance from Ballengeich.

Great Hall or Parliament House 1501-1503. John Lockhard, Walter and John Merlioune, John Yorkstoun (masons). Possibly the finest mediaeval secular building in Scotland. Over 120 feet long, it consisted of a raised King's dais at the southern end, flanked on both sided by rectangular, full height, projecting oriel windows, the insides of which are vaulted, the totality rich with exquisite carving and tracery. The remainder of the hall is lit from pairs of large, deep set windows so high in the wall as to act as a clerestorey, below which were hung tapestries. There is some evidence for the existence of a Minstrel's Gallery at the far end. Projecting circular staircases lead to kitchens and cellars below. There are a number of enormous fireplaces.

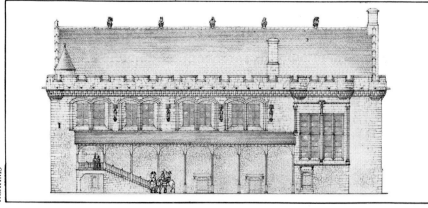

RCAHMS

Above: Stirling Castle Great Hall: conjectural restoration of courtyard facade.
OPPOSITE: conjectural restoration of the interior (courtesy of Scottish Development Department).

The original doors, according to an 18th century traveller, were of oak and covered in bas-relief and *rather old* inscriptions. In addition to being used as a Parliament Chamber, the Hall was the setting for James VI's baptism celebrations for his son Prince Henry in 1594, a detailed description of which survives.

SDD Ancient Monuments

In 1618, the London Water Poet, John Taylor visited the building: *I dare affirm that His Majesty hath not another such hall to any house that he has neither in England or Scotland, except Westminster Hall which is now no dwelling hall for a prince, being long since metamorphosed into a house for the law . . . This goodly hall surpasses all the halls that ever I saw in length, breadth, height and strength of building.*

They who built the castle, wrote Daniel Defoe in 1723 *without doubt built it as the Scots expressed it to continue aye, until somebody should build another there which, in our language, would be forever and a day after: the palace and royal apartments are very magnificent, but all in decay and must be so. Were the materials of any use, we*

THE ABANDONMENT of the Great Hall and later conversion to a riding school, then barracks, led to its decay and the destruction of the original roof — the condition in which Robert Burns saw it, prompting him to pen an incautious squib:

Here Stuarts once in triumph reigned
And laws for Scotland's weal
   ordained
But now unroofed their palace stands
Their sceptre's sway'd by other
   hands.

thought it would be much better to pull them down than to let such noble buildings sink into their own rubbish by the mere injury of time.

The condition of the Great Hall, by now a barracks, attracted Lord Cockburn's wrath in 1845: *How disgraceful it is to the nation and particularly to the Government that the scenes of its history should be converted to such base uses. The place where parliament met a barrack room! and every other sacred spot equally debased!* He would be mollified now. The Scottish Development Department is part way through a painstaking programme of brilliant reconstruction, providing one of the most interesting architectural experiences available in Scotland.

THE EXUBERANT carved statuary of the palace did not appeal to enlightened taste. *It is very rich and curiously ornamented with grotesque figures,* wrote Garnett in 1800, *upon singular pillars or pedestals, each one of which is supported on the back of a figure lying on its breast, which appears a very painful position — especially when encumbered with such a load, and some of the figures seem to wish to be freed of it, if we may judge by the contortion of the muscles of their faces.* In 1802 Alexander Campbell, in search of the picturesque, spotted the *effigy of James V in the highland dress of the times among the statues, if such hideous things in imitation of the human form deserve a name*; and by 1846 the Victorian view as published by Billings condemned the *obscene groups* as the *fruits of an imagination luxuriant but revolting.*

RCAHMS

The Palace 1540-42

In 1539, according to the contemporary historian George Buchanan, *the King, having heirs to succeed him . . . applied his mind to unnecessary buildings.* The result — the great quadrangular palace of Stirling Castle — is one of Scotland's renaissance glories, its most striking surviving feature being the exterior facade. The palace is designed around a central courtyard, known as the Lion's Den (possibly indicating the location of a royal menagerie) of which only the south and north rooms manage to retain anything like their original quality: those on the west were demolished leaving just the gallery, whilst those on the east await restoration. Above a string course, which defines the first floor, the exterior of the palace is identified by a series of gigantic cusped bays within which carved figures rest upon double columns. Above a particularly ornate cornice (cut into by later windows), other smaller columns support yet additional figures. On the apex of the crow-stepped gables is more statuary. The scale of these columns and statuary has to be appreciated: from top to bottom they are several times the height of man. Above each window, which retains its splendid iron grate, is a carved tympanum.

SRO

Top: the Queen's Presence Chamber in the Palace — conjectural restoration.
Above: a new front for the Palace designed from exile by John, Earl of Mar.

OPPOSITE:
Top left: statue thought to be James V in the guise of the Gudeman o'Ballochgeich.
Centre: the exterior of the Palace.

One of the Stirling Heads which once decorated the ceiling of the Queen's Presence Chamber.

RCAHMS

The interior was equally impressive. *The rooms are lofty with carved works on the ceilings* wrote John Taylor in 1618: *the door of each room being so high that a man may ride upright, on horseback, into any chamber.* It became used as a barracks, with officers' quarters above and, when one of the wooden medallions *of exquisite workmanship* fell from the ceiling of the Presence Chamber and injured a soldier, the entire ceiling was dismantled. It consisted of a series of squares within which were set 56 oak medallions, all dating from about 1542, which, after their dispersal, became known as the **Stirling Heads.** Medallioned heads in woods, stone or marble were not uncommon in Europe at that time (a very similar plaster one survives in Craigievar) and the carvers are thought to have been two Scots — John Drummond and Robert Robertson, and a Frenchman — Andrew Mansioun. Most of the heads survive; some are displayed on the walls; and there is a long term plan to restore the ceiling in its entirety. Without the ceilings and the wallcoverings, these gigantic chambers seem bare, their regal scale indicated by the huge window embrasures and stupendous chimneys.

The Chapel Royal 1594.
The Chapel was built at the specific instruction of King James VIth, to replace James IIIrd's Chapel (whose outline is marked in setts in the Square) which was deemed neither large nor elegant enough for the baptism of James's son. *Orders were given to demolish it, and erect on its site another finer. Craftsmen were summoned from all parts of the kingdom; and, that the work might be executed with greater despatch, large pay was allowed and the king acted as daily overseer. The baptism was performed on 30th August with a pageantry surpassing anything of the kind ever seen in Scotland.* It is one of the few ecclesiastical buildings built in Scotland of that date: and is a long rectangular building whose principal windows face onto the courtyard. Internally, it is bare and unfurnished, a major event being the re-discovery of Valentine Jenkin's of 1628-9 *troupe-d'oeil* painted decoration, executed in tempera. The courtyard facade has a plain row of six, double-light round-headed windows, with, at the centre, a fine round-headed doorway framed by coupled corinthian columns supporting an entablature. Little is known about the demolished chapel which lay at an angle in the courtyard save that, according to the

McKean

historian Drummond, James III (builder of the
original collegiate church) was *much given to
buildings and trimming-up of chapels, halls and
gardens, as usual in the lovers of idleness; and the
rarest frames of churches and palaces in Scotland
were mostly raised about this time.* Of all such
collegiate churches, few seem to have enjoyed as
great riches as the Chapel Royal in Stirling,
which had the peculiar distinction that its Dean
was the Queen's Confessor. By 1777, the Chapel
had been turned into a storehouse, but it still
preserved the hull of the boat which James VIth
had caused to be built and placed upon carriages
to be towed into the Great Hall, carrying the
provisions for the baptismal feast for Prince
Henry in 1594. It also preserved the original
pulpit. In the 19th century, the Chapel
continued to be used as a storehouse, finally
being restored earlier this century.

There is much else of interest in Stirling
Castle: notably the **King's Old Building,** a
structure on the northwest side of the upper
square restored in 1857 after a fire by the
antiquarian Robert Billings whose four volume
**Ecclesiastical and Baronial Antiquities of
Scotland** was a major influence in the 19th
century baronial revival. As elsewhere he carved
the detail with his own hands.

From as early as the 17th century, visitors,
travellers and tourists were encouraged to go
round the castle, members of the garrison
supplementing their income as guides *I was met
on the drawbridge by a trim Corporal* wrote
Nathaniel Willis in 1834 *who offered to show me
the lions for a* consideration. *I put myself under
his guidance and he took me to Queen Mary's
Apartments, used at present for a mess room, to
the chamber where Earl Douglas was murdered etc*

RCAHMS

Top: the Chapel Royal from the
courtyard.

Above: the interior, showing
Valentine Jenkins' 1628 trompe
l'oeil decoration.

etc. The pipers were playing in the court. My friend the corporal got but sixteen pence a day, and had a wife and children; but much as I should dislike all three as disconnected items . . . a garrison life at Stirling, and plenty of leisure, would reconcile one almost to wife and children and a couple of pistareens per diem. In 1845 Lord Cockburn took time off from one of his Assize visits: *I never saw the interior of the castle so well before. Seeing it thoroughly now we owed to the politeness of Sir Archibald Christie . . . whose face had the rare honour of stopping a cannon shot, and the still rarer good luck to survive that feat. But the ball has had its revenge. For the convexity of the one cheek and the concavity of the other with their effects, in twisting eyes, mouth and nose, have left as hideous a countenance as war ever produced . . . Except St Andrews, I can't recollect any other place of such exclusive historical interest. They have both been Pompeiid, saved by circumstances from being superseded or dissipated by modern change. It is the old stories along that still linger in each. Stirling has its buildings and its walks, enobled by its singular position; but still, it is the old tales that adorn it.*

Castle Wynd in the 1840s, the complete Argyle Ludging on the left.

McKean

In 1858 the German traveller Theodore
Fontane wrote perhaps the most detailed
description of an intelligent tourist's visit noting,
as Queen Victoria had done before him, John
Knox's pulpit in the chapel, ending upon an
elegiac note *When we went down Castle Hill and
occasionally looked onto the towers and walls and
especially at the picturesquely situated palace,
whose windows were reflecting the red glow of the
dying twilight, another song (bagpipes) sounded
from the castle court and followed us downhill; the
last drum beats echoed away when we turned into
(Friar Street) among whose lights the gas lamps of
the Royal Hotel burned like stars of the first
magnitude.*

2 **The Esplanade** was constructed in 1812 by
D. T. French and the garrison, on land and the
sites of houses and gardens donated by the
Burgh, both to improve the approaches, and to
provide a public place in which the military
parades so beloved of the Victorians could be
staged. Facing it is the **Visitor's Centre**, a
3 brilliant 1971 conversion by Johnston and
Groves-Raines of the 18th century Castle Hotel.
Harled and whitewashed, the windows and doors
emphasised by painted margins, it is enhanced
by a semi-circular entrance porch on the one
side, matched on the other side by three ovoid
smoked-glass oriels billowing from the third
floor, providing visitors with splendid lookout
points. A good view is obtained of the Gowan
Hill with its beheading stone. The immense
height of this narrow building has been exploited
to provide a wide sloping ramp down to an
4 audio-visual amphitheatre. **Mar Lodge,** c. 1817,
looks like a single-storey, pedimented cottage
front built of whinstone and lighter ahslar

View from the Esplanade to the
Wallace Monument and the Ochils.

15

quoins, a fanlit doorway flanked by an Ionic porch: but this entrance is really at second-storey level: its east facade is three storey tall, and has
5 projecting bow windows. The **Portcullis Hotel** is a mid-Victorian conversion of Gideon Gray's 1788 Old Grammar School, a tall plain building, now L-shaped, whose centre bay projects slightly and is capped by a pediment, which may have incorporated some of the stonework of the 15th century Grammar School formerly on this site. Gray was Stirling's first *professional architect* becoming a Freeman of the Burgh in 1769.

6 **Argyle Lodging** 16th century onwards. Scotland's finest surviving Renaissance mansion. It dates from three phases: a 16th century L-shaped tower at the north-east corner, extended east and south in 1632 by Sir Anthony Alexander second son of Sir William, and one of the two Royal Masters of Works; the north-west portion (already extended) was completed in 1633-40, and the south west in 1674. The carved strapwork around and above some of the windows imply the hand of William Ayton, the mason of George Heriot's Hospital in Edinburgh.

THE spelling of "Ludging" or "Lodging" is optional, the former mysteriously antique, the latter prosaic. Both are used in this book.

The Argyle Ludging courtyard.

RCAHMS

McKean

THE PRINCIPAL extensions to the Argyle Lodging in the early 17th century were commissioned by Sir William Alexander of Menstrie, later Earl of Stirling and Viscount Canada as a result of his initiative in the colonisation of Nova Scotia and Northern Ireland. There is much conflicting information about him. He was a considerable poet, powerful courtier and, in 1630, Secretary for Scotland. He failed to prosper, however dying bankrupt and, if the following contemporary rhythme is to be believed, intensely unpopular for issuing debased coinage:

A vain, ambitious flattering thing
Late Secretary for a King;
Some tragedie in verse he penned
At last he made a tragic end.

The street front is closed by a screen wall pierced by a superb, rusticated entrance gateway, and the principal doorway is reached beneath a pedimented porch carried on square fluted columns, capped on the wall behind by an outstanding armorial cartouche outlined in carved strapwork. There are four stair towers, two projecting from the main building, and each capped with a conical turret. Architectural details inside and out — the dormer windows, fireplaces, painted panelling in the upper Hall, the doors and the stair cases are of an immensely tactile quality.

The Lodging was rouped after Stirling's death in 1640, the Town Council thinking to purchase for conversion to almshouses. Archibald, 9th Earl of Argyle bought it in 1666 from whose family derives its name and its 1674 improvements. About 1800 it was transformed into a military hospital. Although still in Crown ownership, it is now a youth hostel.

Above: Argyle Ludging.
Below: Mar's Wark: Gateway to pend.

Mar's Wark 1570-1572

The ruins of a splendid Renaissance palace of exceptional interest whose survival is due, it is said, to the fact that it acts as a buffer against the winds roaring down Broad Street. Its long, two-storeyed facade is focussed on a great arched pend flanked on either side by octagonal turrets built of beautifully cut stone. The importance of the first floor is signified by the presence of a string-course, above which appear most of the carvings, armorial panels, and gargoyles — save the principal archway on the ground floor which is flanked by the remains of columns capped by

McKean

RCAHMS

Above: Mar's Wark.
Below: Heraldic Panel.

Carved panel above the Central Doorway

MAR'S FICKLENESS earned him the nickname of Bobbing John in one of the Jacobites' more scurrilous rants: *Came ye o'er frae France?* which concludes:
Hey for Sandy Don
Hey for Cocalorum
Hey for Bobbing John
And his Highland quorum!
Many a sword and lance
Swings at Highland hurdie;
How they'll step and dance
O'er the bum o' Geordie!

a pediment; and is currently closed by a quite beautiful Arts and Crafts wrought iron gate. The composition is clearly that of a gatehouse and the 1672 drawing by Slezer implies a three-storey building with conically-capped towers dominating the centre. Equally clearly, it was not a gatehouse in the normal sense of the word, the towers simply containing stairs leading to the great rooms on the first floor. The original house is often thought to have been of a courtyard plan, and therefore left unfinished, but the rise in the hillside make it extremely improbable that a full courtyard could have been attained. The quality of the sculpture led to a persistent but unverifiable rumour that the work was built of stones from Cambuskenneth Abbey. Daniel Defoe who visited it in 1723 thought it *too near the castle; and was the castle ever to suffer a close siege and be vigorously defended, the house would run great risques of being demolished on one side or the other.* He was proved right during the 1745 rebellion.

The family of Erskine, later Earls of Mar, is one of the most significant in Scots history, Sir Robert Erskine having been appointed hereditary Governor of Stirling Castle by King David Bruce in 1360. His descendants acquired the Earldom of Mar and lordship of Garioch by marriage, both being confirmed in 1562 to John, Lord Erskine. About 1569 he began the construction of his great Wark, an early instance

of the predilection of the Mar family for architecture; and in 1571 was appointed Regent of Scotland. His death in 1572 was as a result of a *vehement sickness. Some of his friends, and the vulgar, suspected he had gotten wrong at his banquet at Dalkeith from the Lord of Mertoun.* His descendants continued to rise in favour until the Civil War when Mar joined the Marquis of Montrose (another great Stirlingshire nobleman) on the Royalist side, his estates being plundered as a result. His son, after the Restoration, became a Privy Councillor and founded the Royal Scots Fusiliers in 1678. His son John, the 11th Earl of Mar was a successful politician under Queen Anne, rising to be Secretary of State, being all the more aggrieved at his subsequent neglect by the Hanoverians after their arrival in 1714. One of his contemporaries noted of him: *although a time-serving self interested person who could at any time be bought and sold. Of this the Court was well aware, but neglected to secure him to its interests.*

He led the Jacobite rebellion to its inconclusive finale at Sheriffmuir, but seven miles to the north, and died in exile in 1732.

THE WARK played a considerable part in the defeat of the Hamilton (Queen's) forces when they invaded Stirling in early 1572 with the intent of capturing and killing the principal noblemen of the Regent Lennox party. Security was lax, and the Hamiltons secured the entire town — until the common soldiers began to disperse for plunder:

Upon this, John Erskine, Governor of the Castle, who had before tried to break through the enemy in the market place, but in vain, they were so strongly posted, sent a party of musketeers into his own new house; which was then building, and not quite finished, from whence there was a prospect into the whole market place. This house, because it was uninhabited, and not completed, was neglected and afforded a safe post to the Royalists, whence to play upon their enemies; when the rebels saw that they were shot at from a high place, garrisoned against them, with unusual weapons, they presently turned their backs, and ran away in such fear that, when they came to the narrow way leading to the gate, they trod down one another. That which saved them was, there were but few to pursue; for they who had driven them out of the market place could come out but one-by-one through the gate of the new house. Nonetheless, the Regent was shot in the back and died the same day. His replacement was John Erskine, Earl of Mar.

Above: Motto from Mar's Wark.
Left: elevation of the facade by J. S. Fleming (1897).

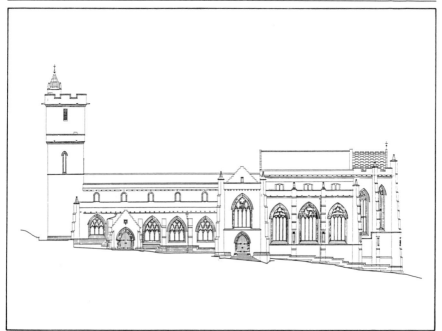

Top: Holy Rude Church: drawing by Honeyman Jack and Robertson.
Above: exterior from the churchyard.

8 **Church of the Holy Rude** from 1456. One of Scotland's most splendid mediaeval parish churches, cruciform in plan and dominated by the tower against its west gable. The **Nave** and tower — though much mutilated — date from 1456-70, traces of the original western doorway still visible from the outside surviving the ghastly 1818 depradations of James Gillespie Graham who filled in the western doorway and lowered the window above. The church has vaulted aisles and one of Scotland's few surviving mediaeval timber roofs up to the centre, or crossing — whose immense masonry piers provide evidence of the builders' original intention for a central tower. The nave is horizontal in emphasis, the cusped tracery of its windows of particular interest. Of the several *aisles* (chapels) donated by merchants, only **St Andrew's Aisle** survived the Gillespie Graham surgery, still retaining today its ribbed vault with armorial bosses, piscina, and peculiar trio of zig-zagged string courses on the exterior. The Crossing, the site of the Holy Rude itself, was *restored* to its current condition by James Miller in 1936: that is to say, it is a correct representation of what the mediaeval masons might have intended but never completed, and later obscured by the insertion of a wall dividing the church into two totally separate ministries.

RIAS Library

Holy Rude Church: 1928 drawing by James Millar, showing the proposed restoration of the interior as it was carried out.

Below: the Martyrs' Monument, Argyle Ludging and the Ochils in the background.
Bottom: Holy Rude chancel by R. W. Billings.

McKean

The emphasis of **The Choir** is determinedly vertical. Begun in 1507 (along with the completion of the west tower) it is altogether a more flamboyant piece of architecture, whose vertically proportioned windows and tracery, vaulted aisles and more slender proportions — are enhanced by the piers of clustered shafts. The presbytery itself is barrel vaulted in ribbed stone, the wall shafts ending in curiously carved heads. Viewed from downhill in St John Street the ensemble, supported by its stern pinnacled buttresses conveys the impression of immense strength.

9   The **Valley Cemetery** was laid out as an extension to the Kirkyard in 1850 on ground once thought to be a tiltyard, and later the horse fair. It is principally of interest for its setting and the views to be had from it, but the **Martyrs Monument** (1858) to Margaret Wilson and Margaret McLachlan is a macabre octagonal glass domed tube enclosing two marble girls in memory of two Presbyterians drowned in Wigtown in 1685; and the **Star Pyramid,** of the same date, with marble statues by William Barclay, both testify to their creator's (William Drummond) preoccupation with mortality.

Above and right: Cowane's Hospital.

10 Cowane's Hospital, now Guildhall
1639, John Mylne
A very good hospital thought Daniel Defoe in 1723: E-shaped in plan, the Guildhall symbolises much of the better 17th century Scots architecture of the middling sort. Two- and three-storeys in height, this part-harled building is distinguished by its tall slenderness, its lower, crow-stepped side wings, and the commanding four-storyed tower through which lies the entrance. The south east gable has a fine, later, window which, together with the rear south west windows, date from the reconstruction of the building into a Guildhall by Francis and William Mackison, in 1852. Above the door is a niche with a dumpy statue of the founder John Cowane, who left 40,000 marks for the *succor of 12 decayed Gildbrother*, his trustees discovering in the early years of the charity, a marked reluctance of Guild Brothers to be thus classified as decayed by taking up one of the places. There are pediments above each window, and the dormer window heads have carved balls for finials. Mackison's Guildhall, formed by taking out a floor and enlarging the rear windows, runs double-height the entire length of the building, overlooked by both balcony and gallery. Cowane's superbly carved 1636 oak chest remains within. The elegant **Bowling Green** — a beautiful urban space — was formed in 1712.

The Guildhall cannon were made at nearby Carron, exported to Russia, and recaptured at Sebastapol in 1855.

THE STATUE of John Cowane has acquired its own mythology. Parents told children that when he heard the last stroke of midnight he came down to dance in the courtyard. The fact that he did not was explained by the fact that the centuries of tolling bells had rendered him deaf.

Swan

The Town Wall 1547

The Town Wall showing the gunpowder bastion.

The south west ridge of the rock was lined from castle to the Barras Yett (where Port Street now is) with a stone wall, which then curved round the bottom of the town to another bastion (preserved in the Thistle Centre). Although there was a gate in St Mary's Wynd, the north east front was fortified by garden walls only, the incline and the marshes of the Forth being thought to be adequate defence. What survives today probably derives from the Council's decision in October 1547 to spend money upon *the strengthing and bigging of the walls of the toun, at this present peralus tyme of neid, for resisting of our auld innimeis of Ingland.* It is best seen from the lovely **Back Walk,** which begins in Dumbarton Road and continues up and round the rock at the foot of the wall, continuing, eventually, right round the base of the castle to Ballengeich. The walk, the happy idea of W. Edmonstone of Cambuswallace in 1723, provides some of the finest views in Scotland. In general, the town wall is constructed of huge whinstone boulders mortared into the rock itself, up to 5' thick at the bottom, rising to a height of 23' in places. There are some crude gunloops. The domed, circular bastion at the rear of Allen's School, has been used both for a dovecot and the storing of gunpowder, and the remains of the Port Street bastion is entombed in the Thistle Centre (see p. 42).

The King's Knot from the Castle, showing the King's Park behind.

<small>Swan</small>

The King's Knot

Known locally as the *cup and saucer*, these pleasure grounds probably date from 1628 when the gardener William Watts was paid for the *platting and contryveing his Majesties new orchard and garden.* The earliest surviving view dating from 1673, shows geometric shapes outlined in box hedges, with ornamental trees planted within each. Thereafter the Knot, like much of the King's Park was let to grazing, the tenants trying from time to time to exclude the public and plough up the garden, thus earning the obloquy of Lord Cockburn in 1842: *The Commissioners put this ground, with all the green and regular mounds which marked its ancient uses as a place of royal and public past-time, into a farmer's lease, and the plough had begun its devastation when public clamour instructed the Commissioners, and they are now in the course of getting their error corrected . . . The fearful fact however, is that such errors can be committed.* The King's Knot, as it survives today, consists of two gardens, the easterly being raised, in octagonal shapes, the westerly being sunk, much fainter, consisting of inter-penetrating squares. Nearby is **The Butts Well** commemorating the archery target area. In 1698 John Allane was paid £24 for a silver box *sett out be the toune as a prize to be shoot for at the Butts by archers.*

12 **Market Place**
The reason for breadth and splendour this *great street* was its former role as the market place since 1226 and the focus of the entire Burgh; and it still commands a spacious grandeur which, on an autumn's evening, is filled with blowing leaves, memories and ghosts. Credit is due to those who have attempted to save both the historic buildings, and the population, of the upper Town, beginning originally with Sir Frank Mears, followed by the Burgh's architect Walter Gillespie. But the concentration upon houses and flats, to the exclusion of any commercial life, has had the result of making the upper Town something of a desolate, single class dormitory, desperately needing the infusion of, say, students or young people to bring it to life once more.

Mercat Cross
All that survives of the historic cross is the finial, in the shape of a sitting Unicorn (known as the Puggy) proudly displaying against its breast the Lion Rampant of Scotland surrounded by a collar of the Order of the Thistle. The Cross was removed in 1792 to ease traffic movement, and was re-created in 1891 on a base of four circular steps.

13 **Tolbooth or Town House** Sir William Bruce 1703-5
In March 1702 the Town's mason Harry Livingston was dispatched to Kinross House to obtain a *draught or scheme of the work* from Sir William Bruce (architect of Holyrood House and former Royal Master of Works) for the rebuilding of the ruinous Tolbooth already on that site. He designed a tall, narrow, 3-bay building with a projecting, square tower at the north western end, whose main stairs lead over the roof of the prison cell, directly into the superbly panelled first floor chamber. The tower is capped by one of the few surviving ogee-shaped Dutch pavilion roofs. The Market Place facade is faced with fine ashlar, with string courses, architraves and a cornice: the Gaol Wynd facade is left in rubble. In 1785 Gideon Gray extended the Town House by three bays to the east in such careful detail that it is barely possible to detect the original from the extension.

McKean

Top: Broad Street from the top showing the Darnley House at the bottom.

Above: Broad Street from the bottom showing the Tolbooth on the left.

BROAD STREET

RCAHMS

Broad Street

Broad Street retains a serene homogeneity of townscape even though the buildings themselves span three centuries. Apart from the Town House, little of note survives on the south west side save **no 39,** a pleasingly classical early 19th century house with keystoned doorway and a modern circular stair tower; and the adjacent **no 41,** which extends round into Kirk Wynd, designed in sympathetic 17th century Scots by Sir Frank Mears, 1937, re-using a moulded ogival panel rescued from the now demolished Lawrie's turnpike. The north-eastern side presents a fine downhill sweep of buildings all at least one storey lower than Edinburgh's Royal Mile counterparts, beginning with **Mar Place House** a simple, classical early 19th century two-storey house with tripartite windows and

·Street·
·Front·
·Broad·
·St·

Above: Northern elevation of Broad Street, drawn by Sir Frank Mears.
Right: James Norie's Lodging by J. S. Fleming.

26

raised quoins. **No 26** is an early 18th century, tall land with arched pend, stair tower at rear and adjoining gate piers; no 24 may be earlier, a storey lower and one bay wider. **20-22** is elegantly stone fronted, distinguished by its ground floor consisting of a huge arched doorway flanked by symetrical, rectangular recessed windows, like a venetian window. **No 18** consists of two buildings: uphill, a plain four-storey, 17th century harled house: downhill, the lodging of **Graham of Panholes** a very distinguished harled block dominated by two crow-stepped gables to the street; the current pedimented doorway a modern innovation, replacing the original central one, when the whole was rehabilitated by Walter Gillespie 1958-9. When in Edinburgh, compare 11-15 Canongate.

14 **Town Clerk James Norie's Lodging** (no 16) would not look out of place in Amsterdam. Dating from 1671, its crow-stepped gable is centred in the facade like a Gothic pediment, the entire front faced in good, well cut ashlar blocks; each window is capped by a crude pediment enclosing the initials and incised Latin texts including *a good conscience is a brazen wall;* and the entire composition is propped up on two facetted (diamond-cut) columns which support the entablature on which the upper storeys rest. The composition made better sense when the ground storey contained large doorways, rather than the three small windows required by the reconstruction. Behind **12-14,** a pleasantly refaced Victorian building with architraves and cornices, **Provost Stevenson's Lodging** — a 17th century harled wing, with a crowstepped stair tower on the corner and round-headed dormers, runs along the close.

Mears

McKean

Bow Street

Once a major cross route, linking St Mary's Wynd, across the base of Broad Street and across the top of Baker Street, to St John Street. It was narrow, as Queen Victoria found out: *Turning out of the lower end of Broad Street by the narrow Bow Street the Queen might have supposed the next move of the horses would be up some turnpike stair so little does it resemble a passage for carriages.* The sturdy four storey 17th and 18th century tenements facing down Baker Street have been replaced by a weak, red and yellow stone, 2-storey confection complete with corner turret by Walter Gillespie, in a form lacking the necessary punch and sense of spatial enclosure.

Top: Bow Street in 1930 from St John Street.
Above: Bow Street now from the bottom of Broad Street, the tower of the Old High School in the distance.

Right: Darnley's House drawn by J. S. Fleming.

Below: Moir of Leckie's Lodging in 1850.

15 No **16-18 Bow Street** is commonly called **Darnley's House.** Following the legend that he resided therein close to, but maintaining his distance from, his wife in the palace uphill. Properly Erskine of Gogar's, the house is late 16th/early 17th century, a tall 3-bay stone-faced, crow-stepped land, two of whose three dormer heads have a triangular head, the third, off beat, being segmental. **Moir of Leckie's** Lodging, behind, 1659 is an L-plan building with early 18th century Venetian windows on 2 floors looking out east over the gardens, orchards and marshes noted by travellers as, for example, Robert Billings in 1846 *The town is full of old houses with paved courts and arched entrances, from which pleasant gardens, wherein we may notice the antiquity of the fruit trees, stretched down on either side of the descent crowned by the castle, and exhibit in a considerable vitality the economy of the old Scottish towns where the houses were huddled together on an eminence, while all round them the gardens of the citizens stretched fanlike to the sun and the pure air.* The rebuilt 18th century Venetian windows on 2 floors Stirlings of Keir, from which their own mansion (see p. 78) could be spotted on its bluff across the Carse.

McKean

St John Street

Together with Spittal Street, **St John Street** used to form part of the long Back Raw (or Row); the subordinate street to Broad Street and the Nether Wynd (Baker Street). A few isolated monuments persist the finest, at the top next to the Bowling Green, being the house of **Bruce of Auchenbowie** (39-41) the town house of Bailie Robert, first of Auchenbowie, which may date from 1520, although much mutilated since. It has a vaulted basement, entered separately from the street as was normal; rendering the first floor the primary level of the house. Note particularly the moulded entrance doorway to the tower; and the large Netherlandish crow-stepped gable downhill. At the corner of Jail Wynd the **Boys' Club, no 36**, is a commendable 1929 reconstruction by Eric Bell, perhaps re-using original walls, but with new crowsteps and the traditional technique of panels with mottos, such as *Play the Game* and *Keep Smiling*.

35-37 is a plain 18th century building on the site of the mansion of **Adam Spittal of Blairlogie,** the superb doorway to which is re-used in the High School extension (see p. 32).

No 33 is rather grander, a mid 18th century house with projecting classical porch (Tuscan) and a pediment. Across the street is the plain, classical **Gaol and Courthouse**, 1806-11, linked to the rear of the Tolbooth and added by Richard Crichton, who, his service being too expensive, was supplanted by messrs Oates, Bowie and Traquair, who probably used his design. The main entrance to the building is up

Top: St John Street, Bruce of Auchenbowie's house on the right. **Above:** Stirling from the King's Park — an etching by Eric S. Bell.

ERIC BELL was a Stirling architect and artist. His etchings show his affinity to Sir David Y Cameron whose close friend Bell was. Cameron considered Bell the better artist of the two, and gave him many of his own originals. Bell kept them in a basement and was known to kick *that rubbish* when asked about them. He was primarily a craft architect, and was founding President of the Stirling Society of Architects in 1933.

a flight of steps to the side, the ground floor windows enclosed within arched recesses, with somewhat vulgar fan-light.

The forbiddingly castellated crenellated gatehouse opposite with enormous ornamental arrow-loops, leads to the currently derelict, equally castellated **Military Prison,** designed in 1847 by Thomas Brown as the County Jail. Its galleried interior was controlled from a domed guardhouse.

Below *from left to right:* the Erskine Church; the Ebenezer Erskine Monuments; and the Military Prison on the right.

RCAHMS

Above: the demolished Fleshers' Tavern, showing the projecting circular staircase typical of old Stirling.

17 **Erskine Church** (Marykirk)
1824-6 Allan Johnstone
Built on the preaching green behind the original chapel, the grand classical church with its pediment and pilasters was a symbol of the rising fortunes of the Seceders. The interior was acoustically perfect, and had a curved gallery, tiered seating and fine plasterwork. It was abandoned in 1968, and set on fire in 1980. Little more than the facade now remains. At the centre of what used to be the elegant front garden to this church is the 1859 **Ebenezer Erskine monument**, designed by Peddie and Kinnear to cover the site of Erskine's tomb in the predecessor church. Square in plan, and rising on Corinthian classical columns to a dome above it seems a peculiarly establishment memorial to a man celebrated and remembered for his stand against the establishment. The name Marykirk derives from the 1934 merger between the Erskine, and the mission church in St Mary's Wynd.

Left: James Maclaren's extension to the Old High School.

Immediately below the Erskine Church is a post-war **cul-de-sac** of two and three storey houses and cottages in the Scots style modified by Festival of Britain picturesqueness, revealing the hand of Walter Gillespie. Part pinkish rubble, part harl, with corbels, crowsteps, mouldings and modern armorial panels, this scheme shows a sensitivity to location 20 years before its time; only marred by the very wide scale, and the lack of enclosure.

Nothing now survives of the pioneering Thistle Property Trust, founded in 1927 to recondition the ancient houses in St John Street, instead of demolition. The 20-year life of the Trust was influential in ensuring that some inherent character, at least, should survive at the top of the town, and demonstrating that rehabilitation was as viable as redevelopment. Occupying the entire frontage of Academy Street between Spittal Street (for such has the Backraw now become) and the Town's Wall is

18 the **Old High School** designed in 1854-6 by J. H. W. and J. M. Hay of Liverpool in a heavy, Gothic manner. The main entrance to the court, beneath a two-storey oriel window supporting a brisk sculpture of children by Handyside Ritchie, is flanked by wings with double-height windows rising into triangular dormers. Down Spittal Street, however, is an extension of an

EBENEZER ERSKINE became minister of the Holy Rude's Third Charge in 1731 and took exception to the re-enacted law 1712 which asserted the rights of the lay patrons to appoint ministers. From 1733 onwards, Erskine refuted that right. *I can find no warrant* he wrote, *from the word of God to confer the spiritual privilege of his House upon the rich beyond the poor; whereas by this Act the man with the gold ring and the gay clothing is preferred unto the man with the vile raiment and poor attire.* The Town Council, Guildry and Incorporated Trades backed him, in 1738 sending five of their number of Perth to *give Mr Erskine what countenance and assistance they can.* In 1740, he was deposed from the West Church and, with several other colleagues, established the first Secession Church, known originally from its site as the Backraw Kirk. In 1747, the Seceders split amongst themselves over the propriety of taking the Burgess oath, those in favour known as Burghers, and those against as anti-burghers. The latter's congregation eventually founded the Viewfield Church. The burghers, in turn, split between two further sects — the auld lichts, and the new lichts. One cannot help wondering if it were not this atmosphere which drove Theodor Fontane, in 1858, to write of Stirling: *a Sunday in Stirling is for the traveller like a thunderstorm at a picnic. You get wet, you can't go on and all your good humour vanishes. We had seen all the sights of Stirling and were horrified at the thought that for the next 24 hours we should have nothing to entertain us but an old copy of The Times and the silent table d'hote. Fortunately, an early train had mercy on us which took us to the ancient City of Perth.*

Above: the Old High School — original drawing.

Below: Spittal Street from King Street showing the Old High School Tower, and the commanding position of the Holy Rude Kirk at the top.

McKean

altogether grander quality, added by James Maclaren (and completed by Robert Watson) 1887-90. Its most striking feature is the four-storey tower with green domed, revolving observatory gifted by Sir Henry Campbell-Bannerman. Its spectacularly carved, cusped archway, contains within it the late 16th century ceremonial dorway taken from a house known as the Reservoir and, prior to that, from that of Adam Spittal of Blairlogie just uphill. It is richly detailed with diamond-faced stonework and carved strapwork. The architecture of the extension immediately uphill is vaguely Scots/Dutch Renaissance in style celebrated by three, oversize, floridly carved dormer windows. Maclaren's design was very influential and the treatment of the tower can be perceived in Charles Rennie Mackintosh's later tower for the Glasgow Herald.

SPITTAL STREET

19 **56 Spittal Street,** known variously as *Glengarry Lodge* or the *Darrow Ludging*, is a 16th century building restored by Robert Naismith (partner of Sir Frank Mears) who recorded the construction as he uncovered it: *The roof carpentry appears very primitive, the rafters and upper and lower ties consisting of roughly adzed timbers, the dressing of which in sum amounts to little more than the stripping of the bark. Each truss is marked probably to facilitate erection after a suitable form of prefabrication. Along the Spittal Street front a 9 by 9" wood purlin beam supports the rafters. The slates are fixed by hardwood pegs which protruded through the underside of the sarking. The wood floors are supported by 6" square wood joists. Most of the stone vaulting survives in the basement as in the ground floors of several other Stirling buildings such as Darnley House (36/8 Broad Street), Norie's House, Moir of Leckie's House and Bruce of Auchenbowie's House. Three other interesting items can be seen at Glengarry Lodge; a squint or diagonal embrasure, now sealed off, has been found in a semi-basement which may have been inserted as an observation point covering the back door, or the approach from Bow Street. The original moulded fireplace opening still exists. The principal room on the first floor has been decorated with a richly moulded plasterwork, now badly damaged, and possesses unique internal side sliding window shutters which can still be operated. In a time when walls have been reduced to the thickness of cardboard, the truly substantial masonry of the old houses surprises. In Darnley House the ground*

McKean

floor walls average about 4' thick. In Moir of
Leckie's from 2' to 7'. *The owners and builders
evidently intended their buildings to survive, an
attitude with which modern thought seems to have
little sympathy. (Architectural Prospect 1955.)*

The Darrow Lodging, the town house of Sir
James Darrow in 1521 from whom it took its
name, preserves its projecting, circular stair
tower with conical roof, but oddly Gothicised
stair windows (dating from the period during
which the house did duty as an episcopal chapel)
crow-stepped gables, long flat dormer windows:
otherwise harled with stone margins.

Its neighbour, **Spittal's Hospital** is 17th
century, but the Victorians robbed it of its
projecting staircase and dormer windows, leaving
a long, plain, steep looking building with
irregular windows. When restoring it in 1959
Robert Naismith restored the circular stair case,
this time in stucco, on the older foundations and
harled the ensemble in brilliant white. Apart
from the survival of a part vaulted ground floor,
the principal interest in the home lies in an inset
panel which claims that, *this hous is foundit for
the support of the puir be Robert Spittall Taillyour
to King James the 4 in anno 1530,* illustrating the
message with a pair of tailor's scissors. Although
this building belonged to Spittal's Hospital it is
probable that the panel was removed from the
Nether Hospital (where Irvine Place now is) on
its demolition in 1751.

ROBERT SPITTAL was a
considerable philanthropist. He
also bequeathed lands in trust, to
the Town Council, on behalf of
decayed members of the Seven
Incorporated Trades, and gave part
of his wealth *for building useful
bridges in this neighbourhood,* among
which were the Old Bridge at
Bannockburn, and the Bridge of
Teith, near Doune, which still
retains an inscription to that effect.
It is curious that the two premier
charities of the Renaissance in the
two premier Scots Royal Cities
were founded by two mercantile
servants of the Crown: goldsmith
George Heriot in Edinburgh and
tailor Robert Spittal in Stirling.

C

Top: the classical pavilion now occupied by the Forth Valley Health Board on the left dominated by the Old High School.
Above: Snowdon School.

Two of the cottages at the centre of **Bank Street,** are possibly 17th century. Facing down that street is the **Forth Valley Health Board Headquarters,** 33 Spittal Street. Built in 1825 as the Commercial Bank to designs possibly by James Gillespie Graham, it is a long, low, two storeyed neo-Classical building in cut stone, dominated by its Greek Doric portico. It was converted by Peddie and Kinnear in 1874 to the Royal Infirmary. The adjacent **Snowdon School** is an 1855 Gothic confection by the Hays of Liverpool, with delicate trefoil-headed lancet windows, and a corbelled turret. In 1888 Ronald Walker designed **Allan's Board School**, the third building deriving from John Allan's Mortification, a fine Edwardian baroque building entered at first floor through a finely sculptured double arch at the head of a staircase. The 1963 office block behind the Athenaeum would benefit from immediate total metamorphosis.

Corn Exchange is a modern intrusion, the sole carriage way to breach the town's defences, and the home of two major civic buildings. Previously, it was Corn Exchange Square, the home of a pleasantly undistinguished classical hotel opened in 1838, *for many years the only place of any size where public gatherings could be held . . . On Fair days, the Exchange was crowded from end to end with country lads and lasses engaged in dancing for which they paid a penny a reel; but other halls being built, the Exchange has been practically foresaken (in 1904) except by sales for auction and paltry entertainments.* In 1908, planned to occupy the entire northern side of the new street, the competition winning **Municipal Buildings** were constructed to the designs of J. Gaff Gillespie, of Salmon and Gillespie (subsequently Gillespie and Kidd and, later, Coia). It is a very confident example of Scots Edwardian architecture, the mainly two-storey block disguised to look larger by a central porch with arched door and flanking three storey wings towered à la Holyrood. The money ran out: the south east wing was never completed, reaching only the central porch. After the Second World War, Walter Gillespie added another bay to the original design to the right of the porch, when extending, before launching out into — as he thought — a further extension in as contemporary a mode as Gillespie's had been in 1908. Unfortunately, in this setting and with this neighbour, his flat roofed design looks visually incomplete and the stone panels

McKean

somewhat threadbare. The late Jack Coia, although a noted modern architect, was deeply upset that his firm was not given the opportunity to complete the building to its original design — for which all the work had been prepared. On the other side of the street is the Carnegie-financed 1904 **Public Library** a competition-winning design *in a late phase of Scottish Architecture* by Harry Ramsay Taylor of Lessels and Taylor: an altogether more refined building in a greyer stone, dominated by a turreted corner tower. The character is Scots Renaissance — crow-step gables, dormer windows, with liberal touches of Elizabethan — parapets and mullioned windows, and Greek — an Ionic doorway. Opposite the Atheneum, the

Above: Stirling's Civic Skyline from Allan Park. On the left the Municipal Building showing its tower, and Holyrood frontage. On the right, the tower of the Atheneum.
Below: the public library.

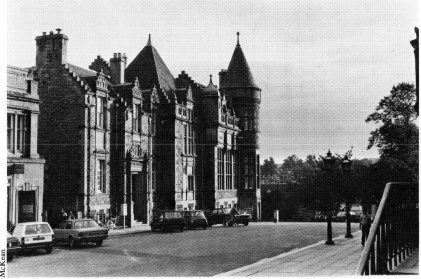

McKean

RCAHMS

23 **Clydesdale Bank,** 1 Corn Exchange Street, 1899 by James Thomson, is a vigorous red sandstone import, very tall, curving round the corner, but uneasy and slightly top heavy. Note how the windows are framed with pilasters, how the first floor is emphasised by a continuous balcony, the rich sculpture above the dormer windows, and the Clydesdale Horse with unicorn's horn which sits, capping the entire edifice, facing the Atheneum.

24 **The Atheneum** 1816.
On the site of the Meal Mercate, the Atheneum was designed by William Stirling, and built by Allan Johnstone. It is a three storey building of well cut stone in a tight curve between Spittal Street and Baker Streets, focussed upon a projecting square tower and spire at the apex facing down King Street; inflicted in 1859, with an amazingly vulgar porch surmounted by Sir William Wallace, sculptured by Handyside Ritchie. The building's original purpose was a merchant's meeting house, with a library and reading room above two shops. The Burgh commandeered it for offices in 1875.

King Street
In ancient times **King Street** was the Meal Mercate, the first great space encountered by a visitor after entering through the Barras Yett, on his way uphill, and out by St Mary's Wynd to the Bridge. It then became known as Quality Street, being christened King Street in honour of George IVth in 1821.

The surviving architecture is principally classical and reasonably imposing, the dominant building, Nos **6-10**, being the 18th century **Golden Lion Hotel**, possibly designed by Gideon Gray. Plain painted with its simple, slightly protruding, pedimented central bay, it was the principal port of call for most Victorian visitors.

King Street, though mostly Victorian, has several classically-styled buildings with details such as pilasters, cornices, and architraves and pediments — particularly numbers 1-15. The **Royal Bank** by Peddie and Kinnear, 1863, somewhat plainer than those architects would normally perpetrate, is an Italianate banking house. The remainder of the south west side of the street is plainly and elegantly classical. The entire street would benefit from comprehensive external restoration to reveal its quality. The **Clydesdale Bank**, early 19th century,

McKean

McKean

McKean

has the customary cornice and architraved windows. **Nos 12-18,** by McLuckie and Walter is a sandstone, shallow detailed building with a wavy balustraded parapet on top and two insignificant conical roofs capping each wing. **Nos 22-24,** 1840 is a symmetrical Italian palazzo, with a splendid row of five pedimented windows on the first floor, and two projecting, balustraded porches with square-columned Corinthian on the ground floor; somewhat in the style of David Hamilton. The classical King Street entrance to the **Arcade,** designed by John McLean 1879-1882, (recently restored by Honeyman Jack and Robertson) was originally a Temperance Hall. The Arcade's interior is particularly rich, the two-storey south west Mall leading to a three-storey central square, with classical details and pilasters which originally contained an upper-floor rustic hall. **Thomas Menzies,** 36-38 c. 1861, is a building of much greater individuality, clearly dominated by its wonderfully vulgar ovoid dormer windows. There is no pretence at classical detailing: this building is an iron-framed structure, all the delight being in the lightness of the structure and the sculptural detail on the walls on either side and the cornice top.

25

Top: King Street showing the Atheneum, the Golden Lion Hotel on the right.
Right: the Arcade.
OPPOSITE top: the Clydesdale Bank, **middle:** Municipal Buildings, **bottom:** Thomas Menzies.

LORD COCKBURN on Circuit in 1852 visited the Golden Lion: *I had rather an alarming entry into that historical city. The magistrates met me at the station, from when we processed to the hotel, them on foot and my lord in his four horse and carriage. But no sooner than had my lord got near the hotel, than the band of the 42nd regiment, a company of which was posted at the door, struck up the sudden crash of drums and pipes, whereupon the unmilitary steeds made a furious and sharp counter-march, and were flying down the steep street, to the horror of the spectators, when, after throwing off the drivers, they were brought to a halt by one of them falling on its side, on which his lordship whisked out by the aid of a Bailie who said good God! the like o' this never happened in the toun o' Stirling before.*

Honeyman   Jack   Robertson

37

Top: Baker Street in 1930, the Bank of Scotland at the bottom. **Above:** Friar's Street showing Hay's Music Shop.

26 The **Bank of Scotland**, designed by William Burn, 1833, is a plain, corner building in excellent stonework, topped with a balustraded parapet. The windows and other details are classical, save for a fine stone fretwork balcony facing Friar's Street. On the opposite corner, is a Germanic, 1900 building by McLuckie and Walter whose dumpy turret recalls contemporary buildings designed for Sir Patrick Geddes in Edinburgh. **Hays Music Shop**, 29-31 Friars Street, 1902 and later altered, is a good example of the idiosyncratic approach of the Stirling architect, John Allan. A four-storey building the centre of which is recessed behind iron balconies, it proclaims its originality with its strident red brick, its stone ashlar dressings, its Art Nouveau details, and manic mottos, which include: *Do yer duty*. **33 Friars Street** is an 1862 stone Victorian building of some detailed quality, its architraves, cornice, scrolls and panels being renaissance in style.

Baker Street runs steeply uphill to Bow Street. Having once been the primary route up into the centre of Stirling and the location of many magnificent ancient buildings, the south side above Bank Street has been removed bringing more light into historic Stirling at the expense of its sense of enclosure. The houses opposite were entirely rebuilt in sturdy Scots by Sir Frank Mears in the early 1930's.

Much of what survives in Baker Street is now of the late 18th/early 19th century. Numbers 10, 12, 14, 18, 24, 26, 28 and 30 are stone-fronted, with plain classical windows, occasionally with added details such as cornice or pilasters at the shop front. On the south side, buildings of an earlier date still survive particularly the 18th century no 13; the early 18th century **Castle Vaults** with steep roof and Elphinstone heraldic panel; 49-53 form an 1891 re-construction of a 1715 house complete with crow-step gables and cornices. Perhaps the finest building in this part of the street is next door, a red sandstone, art nouveau Business Chambers and Tenement, which extends right through to Spittal Street, whose recessed balcony, wavy parapets, art nouveau ironwork, and jettied timber-work betray the hand of McLuckie and Walter, 1900.

27 In a court uphill is **Sauchie House**, 1830, formerly the National Bank but now nursery offices, an elegant, two-storey stone classical building, in its own ground with twin pilasters on either side, architraves above the windows, 28 and a dentilled cornice. **Dalgliesh Court**, 1810,

OPPOSITE top: Baker Street now, **above:** the head of Baker Street post war housing, **bottom right:** Baker Street in 1930, **below left:** Sauchie House.

McKean

now used for the Boys' Brigade is a simple classical house in its own grounds off Baker Street, with a Doric, fanlit doorway, railed steps, and details similar to the houses being built in Melville Terrace of the same period.

The Sir Frank Mears housing comprising the remainder of the street up to Bow Street is high-quality work: some of the buildings pure stone, some harled with stone margins, cartouches with the date above the doorways, some with crow-stepped gables and some Dutch, all in a studied attempt to try to reproduce the accidental picturesqueness of the random buildings which jostle together in historic Scots streets.

McKean

McKean

Mears

St Mary's Wynd

St Mary's Wynd, leading into Upper Bridge Street (or earlier Glencoe Road) was the ancient route from Stirling to Stirling Bridge. Virtually nothing remains of the inner section of this historic route which, about the turn of the century, was so narrow that two carts could scarcely pass in it. Re-development has been harsh, but it is sad that the new buildings were prevented by road-widening lines from fitting their historic setting as they do in the almost identically comparable situation to West Port, Edinburgh.

Most of Lower Castle Hill and Barn Road have been redeveloped but Castle Court contains interesting soldiers' quarters of the late 19th century in great, vigorous stonework and ranks of sturdy chimneystacks. In **Crofthead Court** there is a small group of earlier houses with crow-stepped gables, a rare survivor of the buildings that used to cluster in the area, possibly part of an ancient route up Glencoe Road to Ballengeich and the north postern of the castle.

Above: house formerly in St Mary's Wynd.

Right: John Cowane's House in 1860. It could still be restored to this condition.

McKean

John Cowane's House 1603 onwards.
A substantial U-plan house, built by the man who mortified the Guild Hall. With its pointed turrets, projecting staircase, carved dormer windows and crow-stepped gables it must, in size and quality, have been the grandest commoner's house in the Burgh. It fell derelict in the mid-Victorian times and is now preserved as a monument rather than being restored as it deserves. The house abuts the 17th century

Palace Inn. **The Settle Inn**, 1733 (formerly Red Lion), at the corner of Barns Road, is white painted, crow-stepped building, bearing the legend *Stirling's oldest house*. **Number 9 Upper Bridge Street**, late 18th century, has a classical porch; **no 11**, 1824, a columned fanlit doorway; and **no 15**, St Mary's Roman Catholic Presbytery, a pedimented facade with an oculus, and a fine walled garden. The south side begins with a pleasant old stone malt barn, perhaps part of the vanished Burden's Brewery, used by the Scouts since the 1920's, followed by mainly early 19th century classical terraced houses of which **nos 48** and **50** have particularly interesting doorways. Number 48, pre-1820, was built for the espiscopal Bishop George Gleig, a notable theologian, author and one-time editor of part of the third edition of the *Encyclopaedia Britannica*.

31 **St Mary's Church** 1902.
Peter Paul Pugin (of Pugin and Pugin).
A red sandstone barn whose gable of high quality tracery faces down Queen Street. The stone is heavily coursed rubble, the windows and doors in well carved ashlar, and the interior a quality one would expect.

Above left: Upper Bridge Street.

Above right: 9 Upper Bridge Street.

Left: St Mary's Church. The aerial view on page 2 shows this part of Stirling in great detail.

McKean

Port Street

The site of the Town's main gate, commemorated by brass studs in the cobbles — the Burgh's (later Barras), Yett (later Port). Despite later redevelopments and widening, Port Street retains a different character from Murray Place which continues it — because the old route turned uphill into King Street and Murray Place is a Victorian creation. Much of the east side of Port Street is late classical in style — nos 25-27, and nos 65-69 showing a variety of the usual design features — stone frontages, occasional architraves, pilasters, cornices and (behind **no 75**) a cobbled courtyard at the rear. The **Thistle**

32 **Centre** (1973-76 Walter Underwood and Partners) occupies the lands of former Kinross Coachmakers; and has preserved the Port Bastion of the town wall within it. A 1914 building by E. Simpson leads into **Upper Craigs**, now mostly a traffic route, which represents the old approach from the east.

33 **Craigs House**, pre-1820, is a quality, classical suvival, capped with a balustrade, fronted with a Doric porch and fanlit doorway, all in well cut stonework and added panels of scallop pattern. **Gourlays**, 57-59 **Upper Craigs**, 1935 by John Begg, is a round-cornered brick building on the very corner of the main road, its red brick and long sweeping windows in keeping with the streamlining of the time. **Wellgreen Car Park**,

34 off Upper Craigs, houses **St Ninian's Well**, a rectangular, barrel-vaulted well with washing troughs built by Robert Henderson in 1737, replacing a mediaeval one. Wellgreen was where plague victims were buried.

THE UBIQUITOUS Lord Cockburn had an eye for wells also: *The two or three public wells are all so constructed, having only one spout each that the poor people are obliged to stand idle and shivering for hours before they can get their vessels filled, to their great discomfort and not at all to the improvement of their manners or morals. I counted about 200 tubs, pails, pitchers, etc arranged on the street, with the owners waiting their turns from the solitary spouts. I told the Provost that if I was in his place, these evils should be remedied in a month, simply multiplying the spouts at the existing drawing places.*

Above: Port Street.
Below: Gourlay's.

McKean

Woolworth shares two buildings: a 1906 red sandstone building with traces of art nouveau by McLuckie and Walter, and the 1924 *moderne* building by William Priddle in Woolworth house style.

80 Port Street, the outermost building on the west side, dates from 1770's, a pleasant two-storey house dignified by a pediment, cornice urns and a moulded doorway. **Thomas Elder's**, 1901, by John Allan, is a surprisingly gracious essay in the Queen Anne style popularised in England, distinguished by its two two-storey, flat-fronted bay windows. Number 42, the **Wolf's Craig building**, 1897-8 by John Allan, was designed as a grocer's shop with all the trimmings — a steel frame, its own electricity generator and Welsh bricks. The wolf (whom, legend has it, saved Stirling by barking at Norse invaders and wakening the sentinels) may be seen carved in his niche, and the corner is capped by an unusual hat-like roof supervised by heraldic beasts. The **Nationwide Building Society**, on the opposite corner is a 1901 late classical building by E. Simpson, complete with urns, little pediments and much sculpture, **10-18 Port Street** comprise a succession of mid-19th century classical buildings with pediments above the windows, good proportions and cornices.

Above left: Craigs House.
Above: Port Street and Thomas Elder's.

Murray Place

In the early 19th century, the main route up through the town to Stirling Bridge had become too steep, too uneven, and too narrow to cope with the growth in traffic. From 1824, drovers were permitted to use Mill Street and nine years later both Port Street and Mill Street were widened accordingly. Murray Place was feued in

1842, named after William Murray of Polmaise, who had been instrumental in its formation. The subsequent arrival of the railway at that side of town confirmed it as the commercial hub of Stirling. It was considerably grander than the over-trafficked route it has become today, being an opulent space lined by Victorian mercantile or religious buildings whose quality would be better appreciated by cleaning the buildings and paving the roadway.

The **Bank of Scotland** on the corner of King Street, was designed in 1862-3 by J. W. H. and J. M. Hay, the Liverpool architects better known for their scattering of Free and Episcopal churches throughout the length and the breadth of Scotland, as the premises of Drummond's Stirling Tract Depot — the hub of an extensive pyramid-selling operation of religious tracts. Entered through a splayed corner, it is a grandly sculptured stone Italian palazzo, a balustrade at first-storey level, heavy hoods and pediments above the windows, the proportions being emphasised by prominent cornices.

35

The **South Church**, 67 Murray Place, 1851-53, is a design of soaring elegance by the Hays of Liverpool, a dramatic gable reached up flights of steps from Murray Place, its spire one of the landmarks of Stirling. **77-79 Murray Place**, 1872, (originally the Commercial Bank) by David Rhind, is wealthy Italian Renaissance, emphasis as usual on the first-floor windows, (although the original balcony facing Murray Place has been removed), the corner with Friars Street emphasised by quoins, and the entire building dignified by a balustrade. **The Baptist Church**, 1854 by William Mackison is more like a Jacobean toy, its elegantly slender front consisting of a principal gable capped by an ogee-roofed cupola, with side bays each with a shaped gable capped by a finial. **80-82 Murray Place**, 1854 by J. Dick Peddie in banker's Italian, is squeezed between its two main, hooded and consoled doorways, the windows between, and the floor above, being round-headed, squared off by architraves; the whole is capped by a strongly projecting cornice. The

36 **Post Office**, 1895 by W. W. Robertson has verve, the composition emphasised by the end two entry bays being carried right up through to a strongly projecting dormer head.

Murray Place leads into **Barnton Street**, the corner of which with Friars Street is the former **Royal Hotel**, a classical building with cornices, architraves and pediments.

Top: Port Street.
Above: Murray Place with the South Church tower.

McKean

Princes Street

A steep, truncated street, mostly of Victorian villas and terraced houses beautifully built with carved details around doors and windows. The 37 **Drill Hall**, 1892, built as the HQ of the Argyll and Sutherland Highlanders' 4th Volunteer Battalion stands to attention in vigorous Scots baronial style with twin towers.

Irvine Place

A steep hillside of Regency villas, those on the north dated 1835 — good, elegant two-storeyed pavilions with Doric-columned porches. The south side is terraced, but **no 15**, toward the top is a particularly grand three-storeyed house with a pedimented, slightly projecting central bay, like the Portcullis Hotel. **St Mary's Parish Hall** is the 1838 stone predecessor of the Pugin Church at the head of Queen Street. Excellent stonework, miniature turrets, an elegantly shaped Dutch gable and a delightful oculus give the building great charm. The 1923 Salvation Army Hall downhill is a pious imitator.

THE 1835 FEU conditions for **no 2 Irvine Place** were specific. David Stewart was required to build: *a neat dwelling-house and offices of stone and lime, covered with good blue slates, the front thereof to be either of hammer-dressed whinstone or dressed or polished free-stone with regular hewn doors, windows, skews and tops of vents, and shall lay out the remainder of said lot in a garden or pleasure ground. That the dwelling-house shall be built fronting Irvine Place exactly 18 feet back from the front wall delineated on the said plan and shall be not less than 30 nor more than 40 feet in length, two storeys high in front, similar to the houses built in Allan Park by Dr Galliers.*

Left: Princes Street and the Drill Hall.

Below: No 15 Irvine Place.

Left: the houses in Irvine Place built as a result of the above feu conditions.

RCAHMS

McKean

45

44 **Viewfield Church**, 1860 by Francis Mackison, is a fitting exclamation mark at the bottom with its slender spire and vertical proportions. It has lived down its old title of *back-ee-toon anti-burgher meeting house.*

Queen Street from 1820, Allan Johnstone. An object lesson on how to achieve variety within the one type of classical format, since the houses differ from each other in a number of ways, although all within the overall classical pattern. The ingredients include fanlights above the doorways, dormer windows, pediments, friezes, cornices, wall head chimneys and architraves. Despite the apparent homogeneity of the street, few houses are identical. At the head of Queen Street is the graceful intrusion of the former **Queen's Cinema**, 1928, by G. R. Davidson.

Above right: Queen Street.

Above: bottom of Queen Street.

Below: original drawing of the Sheriff Court Building.

Below right: the Sheriff Court as built.

38 **Sheriff Court Building**
Thomas Brown 1864, (original design) modified and built by Wardrop and Reid 1874-76. A tame composition saved by excellent baronial detail, the facade is dominated by the two projecting crow-stepped wings, with fine carved panelling above the first-floor windows. The main block is enlivened by its projecting doorway, and the three rather fantastic, French dormer windows, projecting from the roof. The courtroom contains an impressive hammer-beam

roof, original seating and hooded canopy above the judge's bench.

39 **1/10 Viewfield Place** a good, 1835, classical terrace, consists of two-storey buildings raised above a basement, entered through pilastered doorways with fanlights above.

41 One of Stirling's rare tenement developments was the 1907 enclosure of a Bowling Green (which still survives) by Wallace, Union and Bruce Streets, Wallace being designed by John

42 Allan. The **Clocktower**, Union Street roundabout, 1910, was designed by McLuckie and Walter for Provost Bayne, whilst the Union Street Hospital, 1906, by the same architects, began life as a Peddie and Kinnear poorhouse. It

43 is now the **Orchard House Hospital**, in the grounds of which is a well-scaled orange brick and tiled roofed **Health Centre**, 1982, by Alex Strang and Partners.

Swan

Swan

45 **Stirling Old Bridge**
Probably late 15th century.
One of the finest and most picturesque mediaeval bridges surviving in Scotland, it consists of four semi-circular arches with stout, triangular cutwaters above which there are refuges on the bridge itself. The square, pyramid pillars were added in the 18th century. Clearly this was not the actual bridge on which Sir William Wallace fought the English, but the location of that bridge has never been determined. For centuries, it was thought to have been a timber bridge at Kildean, about half a mile to the west, but an equally convincing case has been made of the site of the current bridge. The arch nearest to Stirling was severed by General Blakeney during the 1745 and rebuilt. **Stirling New Bridge** designed by Robert Stevenson in 1831-2, flatter, and wider is clearly more efficient: thus lacking some of the romantic attenuation of the old one.

Top: the Clock Tower, Union Street.

Above: Stirling Bridge.

Above: Stirling Bridge.

RCAHMS

The Shore

Visitors, more especially those from shipping ports and coastal towns, wrote Drysdale in 1904 *are apt to poke fun at the inhabitants of Stirling concerning the harbour.* Nevertheless, from earliest days Stirling was indeed a small shipping port, although the winding nature of the Forth meant that from the 17th century onwards, large cargoes were transferred from big ships at Bo'ness into smaller ships for the final stage. Shipping traffic in the Forth was further affected by the withdrawal of the water from the Forth and its feeder rivers into the Glasgow water supply. There was a small shipbuilding industry down at the Shore, and in 1852 Mr Johnston launched *The Stirling* (500 tons) and in 1856 *William Mitchell* (1,000 tons). Until the arrival and the dominance of the railways, the fastest method of travel to and from Stirling was by boat. As late as 1845, 100 boats were trading regularly up to Stirling, with two passenger boats a day.

The American journalist Nathaniel Willis recorded the curiosity of a boat race on this winding river in 1834: *with portmanteau and carpetbag from the hotel to the pier, I was at last embarked in entirely the wrong boat by sheer force of pulling and lying. The two rival steamers, the* **Victory** *and the* **Ben Lomond** *got underway together; the former, in which I was a compulsory passenger, having a flageolet and a bass drum; and the other, a dozen lusty performers and most of the company. The river was very narrow, and the tide down, and although the other was a better boat, we had the bolder pilot and were lighter laden, and twice as desperate. Whenever we were quite abreast, and the wheels touched with the narrowness of the river, we marched our flageolet and bass drum close to the enemy and gave them a blast to awaken the* dead, *taking occasion, during our moments of defeat, to recover breath and ply the principal musician with beer and encouragement. The two pilots stood broad on their legs; and although* **Ben Lomond** *wore the cleaner jacket,* **Victory** *had the* varminter *look. You would have bet on* **Victory** *to have seen the man. He was that wickedest of all wicked-looking things, a wicked Scotchman — a sort of saint-turned-sinner. The expression of early good principles was glazed over with drink and recklessness. We were, perhaps, a half dozen passengers exclusive of the boys, and we rallied round our Bardolph-nosed hero and applauded his skilful manoeuvres; sun, steam and excitement together producing a temperature on deck that left* *nothing to dread from the boiler. As we approached a sharp bend in the course of the river I perceived, by the countenance of our pilot, that it was to be a critical moment. The* **Ben Lomond** *was a little ahead, but we had the advantage of the inside of the course and very soon, with the commencement of the curve, we gained sensibly on the enemy and I saw clearly that we should cut her off by half a boat's length. As we came at the rate of 12 miles in the hour sharp onto the angle of mud and bullrushes, to our utter surprise the pilot jammed down his tiller and ran the battered nose of the* **Victory** *plump upon the enemy's forward quarter! The next moment we were going down like mad down the middle of the river and far astern the* **Ben Lomond** *stuck in the mud, her paddles driving her deeper at every stroke, the music hushed, and the crowd on her deck standing speechless with amazement.*

McKean

Stirling Railway Station, Station Road.
James Miller 1913-15.
One of the loveliest of surviving Scottish railway stations, Stirling presents a newly washed, crow-step gabled and crenellated facade to the street. That hides a low, spacious and beautiful concourse, a miniature repeat of Miller's 1905 extravaganza at Wemyss Bay, its gently curving stairs leading across the platforms retaining an Edwardian charm that is all but lost elsewhere. To the Motorail traveller coming from the south, the sight of the castle silhouette high on its rock in the early light of dawn is one of the most exciting ways to enter Scotland.

A number of interesting railway buildings survive to the south east, particularly a now rare survival of a large, signal box, its long, upper-glazed storey cantilevered from its brick plinth.

The Railway Station. The spire of the Wallace Monument can be seen on the left skyline.

46 The **mill/granary building**, off Kerse Road, (to the right just before the telephone engineering centre) is a patterned brick gem whose roofline is punctuated by the gables of two loft entrances.

47 **Forthside House**, Seaforth Place, 1815. Now marooned in an inaccessible Ministry of Defence compound, on the very edge of a bend in the Forth, this imposing two-storey and basement stone faced building has Doric pilasters and a Doric columned porch at the head of a fine flight of steps. The sides are stuccoed and the rear is harled. Cleaned, its grounds repaired, and opened it would be an immense asset to Stirling.

Forth Place, c. 1825. A row of classical terraced houses, each built of well-cut, dark whinstone, most retaining Doric pilastered doorways, some with architraves above the windows, and cornices. Its currently sunken condition is the consequence of the later arrival of a road bridge over the railway requiring embankment. It continues into **Forth Crescent**, which maintains the elegant urbanism, but is generally later, save **28-30** which is not unlike the houses in Melville Terrace, complete with fanlight.

This area is a **cul-de-sac**, marooned between the railway line and the Forth. The views across the river are spectacular, and some of the later housing around Queens Haugh or the Victorian houses in Dean Crescent are very rural.

Top: Robert Wall's Granary buildings, Kerse Road.
Above: Forthside House.
Right: Forth Place.

McKean

The King's Park

The land to the south of the ancient Burgh formed part of the Royal Park until 1506, when the King swapped it for Gallowhills (now the Gowan Hills) after which it became Burgh common land. Its shape was determined by three roads: the new road from Stirling Gate to Dumbarton on which feuing began in 1837. The ancient road to Cambusbarron (Park Road) improved by the military after 1745; and the old road to St Ninian's and the south which was improved to its current split-level state c. 1785. Feuing began just after the turn of the century. The district between Dumbarton and St Ninian's Road must comprise one of the most opulent Victorian suburbs of any community in Scotland, if not Britain, mostly developed after the arrival of the railway for the better-off merchants from Glasgow. Its romantic, sylvan, setting, overlooked by the mediaeval monuments on the crag above, could hardly be equalled.

The first development was Allan Park, almost contemporary with the splendid houses forming Melville Terrace. The second splurge after 1856 was the development of Spittal Park (the Victoria Square area) and Southfield (the Gladstone Place area) largely to designs by Francis Mackison. The final stage was the Glebe area feued by James Ronald after 1879.

Until 1837, the only substantial building (which still survives) was the **Inclosure**, c. 1710, now in Windsor Street — an old Scots house of great charm, with harled walls and fine stone details. The remainder was either nurseries, agricultural, or sand quarrying.

McKean

View over the King's Park to Stirling Castle.
Below: the Bowling Green.

Dumbarton Road and Albert Place

The south side of Albert Place consists largely of 1837-50 classical cottages behind small gardens and wide pavements. A few have pedimented doors or windows, one or two have pilastered doors or bay windows; the corners of one are picked out with quoins; and a few are painted. Nos 10 and 11, flanking Clarendon Place, and 18 and 19 flanking Victoria Place, are much more Victorian asymmetrical, two-storey with barge-boarded gables. No 15, is a grander classical house with a pilastered front, pilastered doorway, and a cornice.

49 **Albert Hall**, a florid, overbearing design of 1883 by William Simpson, uses the round arches of a Venetian palace to distraction, with added pediments and a balustrade.

50 **Holy Trinity Episcopal Church**, Albert Place. Sir Robert Rowand Anderson, 1875-6.
This large church in scholarly 13th century gothic with external details similar to those of Dunblane Cathedral signifies the assumption of the episcopalians to the establishment. Plainly elegant from the outside, although lacking a planned tower, the inside is brick lined, with round-arched bays, a timber wagon roof, and fine craftwork in the pulpit, screen, altar and reredos. Anderson was not pleased that his former pupil, Sir Robert Lorimer, undertook much refurnishing.

51 **Smith Art Gallery**, 40 Albert Place. John Lessels 1872.
Stirling's principal museum and gallery is housed in a deep single-storey building of considerable quality, its street front dominated by a pedimented, Doric columned portico. It extends far back in a series of galleries, the flank punctuated by two projecting gables with venetian windows. The Ballengeich Room features travelling exhibitions. The gallery has a considerable collection of art and Stirling memorabilia. The nearbye diminutive crudely gothic decapitated Bowling Green clubhouse dates from 1866.

42 Dumbarton Road is a large rock-faced Victorian house. **No 30** is elaborately barge boarded; **no 32-34**, 1878 by John Allan for himself, is also rock-faced with bay windows, whilst the corner pavilion with Royal Gardens has pilastered doorpieces, pavilion roofs and a tower, declaring that here the town stops and the country begins.

Top: Dumbarton Road.
Middle: the Smith Art Gallery.
Above: the Albert Hall.

McKean

McKean

52 **Allan Park** 1818-36

An L-shaped development of villas, mostly in dressed stone or hewn whinstone which was *a new departure from the invariable pattern of four-walled, whitewashed or whinstone houses of the 18th century.* The finest are **Wellington Place** (nos 1-9) which predate 1820: a row of six houses designed within a single monumental facade by Alexander Bowie and Thomas Traquair. Some of the details are similar to Craigs House (see p 42) built for Bowie's uncle. No 2-6, opposite, were designed by Bowie on his own, 10 years later. The symmetry, proportion and classical details slightly reminiscent of Samuel Wyatt.

The remainder of Allan Park consists of contemporary two-storey and basement villas, some in whinstone, with fanlights. No 8 is by Traquair, 12-14 by Allan Johnstone and no 24 was possibly designed by William Stirling.

The **Allan Park Leisure Centre**, designed as a cinema in 1938 by Sam Runcie, replaced the first house in this elegant oasis, and was required to conform to its classical location to assuage controversy: hence, presumably, its 53 *thermal* window. The **Black Boy** fountain, 1849, putatively on the site of the Burgh's gallows, was bought from Neilson and Co (Glasgow) and sited by Robert Logan. The **Christie Clock**, 1906, is a design by A. M. Lupton to reproduce a 17th century clock in cast iron on a pedestal to commemorate Provost George Christie.

54 **St Columba's** (the Peter Memorial Church) 1901, by J. J. Stevenson is a fine gothic achievement in elegant stonework, the tower lacking the crown designed for it. Stevenson, a Scot, practised from London, and many of the brighter late Victorian Scots architects tended to use a period in his office as a finishing school before setting up their plates.

Above left: Wellington Place, Allan Park.
Above: the edge of the town by Royal Gardens.
Below: St Columba's Church.

Top: the King's Park from Victoria Place. On the skyline the tower of the Holy Rude, Cowane's Hospital, and the Military Prison. **Above:** corner of Victoria Square and Place.

THESE WERE the houses not of the burghers of a mediaeval market town, but of Glaswegian industrialists and entrepreneurs. At a given time each evening, the housemaid would light the front door lamp, open the door and the gates, and remain in the porch awaiting Master's return by carriage from the station: and thus it was for decades, in each house in Clarendon, Victoria, Balmoral, Abercromby, Windsor, Park, Drummond, Gladstone and Snowdon Places.

Victoria Square, Place, Clarendon Place, Queen's Road

The first large-scale development feued by Mackison — spacious, wide streets, a large sunken central square, and serried ranks of detached and semi-detached stone villas mostly rather douce and well behaved. The corner of Victoria Square and Place is a good example: beautiful stonework, opulent details, and a solidly proportioned two-storeyed house rasied above a basement.

The houses are elegant — mainly two-storey, often rubble with dressed stone quoins, bays rising through two storeys, side pavilions, emphasised doorways, hipped roofs, and grand doorways with a variety of carved stonework, columns and pilasters. **1 Queen's Road**, 1863, by Francis and William Mackison, is rather more vivid than the norm, with elaborate bargeboarding, patterned slates and prominent gables. **Beechcroft**, 17 Clarendon Place has the Italianate tower and balustraded balcony contemporaries christened *Drummondesque* after William Drummond had built his prototype **Rockdale**, in nearby Park Place, in 1855. **7 Park Avenue** is another towered, pedimented doorway mansion with a superb stone billiard room. **Park Terrace**, opposite, offers an even grander array of buildings — possibly the grandest in the entire Park — that on the corner of Gladstone Place being the epitome of the Italian style — a flight of steps leading up to an Ionic doorway at first-floor level of a five-storey tower; although **nos 10-11** is throwback classical — symmetrical, a pediment, fanlight and Doric doorway.

The Glebe from 1879. James Ronald. 3-5 Glebe Crescent is distinguished by a colonnade of square columns across the centre of

the house, whilst nos **12-14** have spired bay windows linked by an ironwork balcony. They lack the authority of Park Terrace. **16-17** Glebe Avenue is Edwardian, with dwarf columns and a sculptured frieze by the main entrance. James Ronald, the builder of those houses and most of the major late Victorian buildings in Stirling, was a noted antiquary, and a Bailie. His *Landmarks of Old Stirling* is a classic of its type.

Cambusbarron Road/Park Place

Park Place has more concentrated atmosphere — high stone walls, cedars and yew trees, stone finials, balls, crockets and gables — than anywhere else in Stirling: probably because the scale is tighter: a landscape pregnant of Conan Doyle mystery. No **39-41** is distinctly Tudor with oriel windows and roll-mouldings, whilst the **Shieling** has a tower with decorative cast-iron balcony. **4 Birkhill Road** is another Tudor effort with high roofs, gables and octagonal chimneys, whilst **Birkhill House**, on the edge of the motorway, is white painted regency Tudor with dormer windows.

Batterflats, Polmaise Road, is a virulent 1897 building by John Allan, red roofs and half-timbering, now used as a rest home. One or two houses in **Dalmorglen Park** are excellent essays in Scots architectural history from about the turn of the century. **Endrick Lodge**, 1899, by William Leiper is a substantial late Scots, Arts and Crafts mansion.

Southfield

Less cohesion in this development. **Gladstone Place** is spacious, **Southfield Crescent** the heart and somewhat grander, and **Snowdon Place** has the best — particularly the towered Italianate **no 9**, the mid-Victorian, French **no 15** with curving screens and outbuildings, and the Jacobean-gabled **no 14**. **Nos 3-5** are in the classical whinstone villa type of Melville Terrace.

Top left: Carlton House, Snowdon Place.
Top: 9 Snowdon Place.
Above: Park Place.

McKean

Above: 6 Melville Terrace.

St Ninians Road and Melville Terrace

No 3 Pitt Terrace is a 1797 prototype, by architect James Miller, of what was to be built in Melville Terrace 20 years later; and nos 5-7 are early 19th century of similar ilk but much altered by the Victorians, with the unusual feature of a protruding semi-circular, two-storey bay.

A very grand procession of 14 classical mansions of two main floors above a depressed basement of the servants' offices, march along **Melville Terrace**, each set in its own grounds each with its own flanking walls and all probably built between 1815-25. Those interested in the variations classical architecture could provide within the confines of a single approach should study these houses. Half are four-window semi-detached houses, and half three-window individual mansions; nine have fanlit doors; several are built from good square blocks of dark whinstone, the remainder being harled or painted (**no 10** refaced in ashlar); eight have pilastered porches, four in Ionic style and three Doric; and the majority have an emphasised cornice. **No 4** is the Terraces Hotel and may be viewed, and **no 5** is the County Club. **13-14**, and possibly **no 6** can be attributed to Allan Johnstone, 1821, although it is a reasonable surmise that he had a hand in the others.

57   **Viewforth**, now headquarters of Central Regional Council, is part modern, by A. J. Smith, County Architect and part 1855 Victorian gothic by J. W. Hay — being one of the original grand villas which lined the escarpment overlooking

the Forth floodplain. It was extended by James Miller, 1936-7, in a frigid, brick Scandinavian-influenced block. The region has now spread

58 into **Langgarth** (nos 13-15) an 1897 mansion by William Leiper and Ebenezer Simpson in 17th century Scots style, signalled by a vivid, cream and red stone, L-shaped, turreted lodge on the main road. The mansion is a stone, Arts and Crafts, English conception, realised with Scots motifs such as corbelled angle turret, a tower with conical roof, and crowstepped gables. There is a pretty brick gazebo in the garden.

59 **Annefield**, 1785, swamped by the arrival of Stirling Albion in 1947, is a large 18th century building, extended in 1913 by E. Simpson and

60 currently needing friends. **Brentham Park**, 1871, is a high Victorian mansion, with conically capped corner turrets, corbelled out from the main block, a semi-octagonal entrance tower with balastraded parapet, projecting bays and high, French roofs, the main one of which, above the entrance, has been truncated (as has

61 been the conservatory). **Westerlands** 1898, by McLuckie and Walter, replaced the ancient 17th century mansion of Wester Livilands, part of a tempera ceiling from which was rebuilt above one of the stair landings in the new house (the remainder going to museums). Reached through well-crafted stone gatepiers and down a wooded drive, Westerlands is dominated by its red roof, fine stone exterior, and given identity by its crow-stepped gables and octagonal tower.

Clifford Road is mid-Victorian, with variations in the use of decorative barge boarding, the variety of the windows and the use of peculiar, incised stone doorways all clearly providing the clients with their money's weight in stone.

Top left: Westerlands.
Top: Central Regional Council offices: a contrast between Langgarth (right) and the new Central Region Headquarters.
Above: Brentham Park.

Right: Royal Infirmary.
Below: Livilands Gate.
Bottom: Randolph Terrace.

Swan

Swan

McKean

62 **Royal Infirmary**, Braehead.
James Miller, 1928.
A pleasant neo-Georgian block with projecting wings, tall chimney stacks at the gables, hipped roofs, and plain pilasters reaching through both storeys. The architect lived in nearby Randolphfield. The corner of Livilands Gate and Bellfield Road hosts a highly crafted part harled, part stone, L-plan house/bungalow, possibly designed by E. Simpson, architect of **23-25 Randolph Road**, c. 1910 — itself a mixture of harling, red sandstone, and half timbering.

Randolphfield, a small 18th century mansion with stable block, is concealed behind an 1878 neo-classical frontage, with pilastered windows and Corinthian columns; itself overwhelmed by
63 the new **Police Headquarters** of Stirling and Clackmannanshire designed by County Architect Alexander Smith in 1973 — in a style appropriate to the new Range Rover image of the constabulary.

64 **Beechwood** Mid-18th century
A two-storey mansion flanked by single-storey wings with 1851 additions by Charles Wilson. It has dormer windows, is currently harled, and is in use as Council offices.
Randolph Terrace is greatly undervalued, the houses just above Kirk Wynd being clearly of the 18th/19th century, some with arched pends to the rear, of the grander urban sort. Just beyond, it has a fine row of single-storey classical cottages with Doric doorpieces.

65 **St Ninians**
An ancient village, locally known as St Ringans, which gives its name to the largest parish in Stirlingshire. In the 18th and 19th centuries, the parish was famous for weaving of tartans and shalloons and for its minerals. *Coal* wrote a gazetteer in 1845 *everywhere abounds . . . of a very superior quality, it burns with a bright flame, emits a great heat, and has very little sulphureous*

McKean

St Ninian's Tower and the Forth Estuary.

impregnation; and it seems to be inexhaustible in quantity. The collieries of Auchenbowie, Bannockburn and Pleanmuir are the most ancient, but new pits are from time to time opened.

Steeple, Parish Church.
Robert Henderson and Charles Bachop, 1734.
The only complete survivor of the ancient church, blown up in 1745 when being used by an inexpert Highland army as an arsenal, although part of the early 16th century chancel, and a capital in the graveyard also remain. A tall, slender design, with dressed stone for corners and outlining windows and doors, it was formerly harled. Its four stages are capped by an ashlar dome, and cupola, flanked by urns.
The Church, 1751, was rebuilt as a plain stone barn, on a separate site to the north, which by 1845 had become *cold, damp and uncomfortable.* In 1937 a considerable reshaping was undertaken by A. M. McMichael, the result being a structure of interest and elegance, in a kind of Lorimerian manner (somewhat impaired by other alterations since). McMichael was a founder member of the Stirling Society of Architects who later achieved the dignity of Provost.

Of the houses, misleadingly recorded as *old fashioned, clumsy and utterly destitute of grace* survivors exist only in **Kirk Wynd**, and a lone cottage marooned by the by-pass at the edge of Shirra's Brae. **Kirk Wynd**, predominantly 17th/18th century, with one wing dated 1629, has been restored in an artificially picturesque manner (ie dressings treated with plastic stone) yet their crowstepped gables, forestairs, roofs, harling and stone margins comprise an unusually comprehensive survival. The **Old Manse**, next door, carries both the doubtful date of 1677, and the crowsteps, harling and plastic stone of its neighbours. The **Church Hall**, 1834-5, is single-storey stone and bellcotted with overhanging eaves.

SIR THOMAS DICK LAUDER'S fawning description of Queen Victoria's first visit to Scotland in 1843, recorded that in *the steep, hollow and narrow street of St Ninians a person in one of the windows dropped a folded piece of paper into the Royal Carriage which fell on the Queen's knee unperceived by Her Majesty. The Prince (Albert), without saying a word, picked it up and threw it over the side very properly providing in this way against the chance of its containing anything offensive. It afterwards turned out to be a piece of poetry in honour of Her Majesty's visit.*

St Ninian's Steeple and Kirk Wynd.
OPPOSITE top: The Brae, Bannockburn, **middle:** the Royal George Mill, **bottom:** Our Lady and St Ninian's Church.

The Church of the Holy Spirit, McGrigor Road, 1964, by the Irish architect Boyd Barratt is distinctive for its highly modelled windows and doors.

Torbrex
A small weaving village of mainly 19th century cottages, in the midst of post-war expansion, whose survival may be due to the absence of a through road. White-harled **no 14** is dated 1756 on the lintel and is an amalgamation of two earlier cottages; whilst **Torbrex House**, 1721, (now the Inn) the only building grand enough to be two storeys, has crowstepped gables, and an armorial tablet; but its ancient stone walls, failing to satisfy contemporary taste, have been refaced. The new **High School**, 1962, by the County Architects' Department, is typical of the period, forming a spacious campus when compared to its predecessor in Spittal Street.

Williamfield House, 1682, and later Victorianised, was built by William Wordie of Torbrex, his initials and those of his wife Jean Mill being in the lintel above the door. Now cream-harled with black gabled and finialled dormer windows, it was the centre of a large estate.

McKean

68 Bannockburn

To those not from Stirling, the existence of a
village, mills and stately home bearing the name
of the great battle seems rather sacrilegious. The
Bannock (or white) Burn used to power the
Wilsons' textile mills, thus causing a great
expansion of this ancient community. The heart
is therefore at the glen of the Burn by the Old
Bridge — formerly occupied by Skeoch's Mill.
The Old Bridge, 1516, spans the river between
The Brae and The Path, (the former main road)
an inscription recording that the bridge was
another donation by *Robert Spittall, Taylor to
King James the Fourth, 1516, repaired in 1731,
1710, and remodelled in 1781.*

RCAHMS

The principal survivor of Bannockburn's
famous tartan industry, mills, dye houses, and
warehouse, is the **Royal George Mill**, 1822,
saved solely because its third storey is now a
Masonic Hall, entered through a suitably
pedimented and decorated gable. Lesser mills
survive upstream.

The Path retains two Georgian houses the
lower of which has a pedimented Doric doorway;
and **The Brae** presents a fine sequence of 18th
and 19th century buildings, scrolled skewputts,
and pedimented doorways. The large, plain, **Old
Schoolhouse**, 1833, may soon be restored for
the National Trust. **Allan Church**, 1838 in the
manner of John Henderson — spired with
Gothic windows — dominates Quakerfield. **Our
Lady and St Ninian's Church,** Quakerfield, is
an extraordinarily graceful, tall, narrow, building
with vivid orange pantiles and bright brickwork,
designed by Archibald Macpherson in 1927.

McKean

View Vale c. 1850, on New Road is a confection of turrets, and dormers whilst the **New Road Bridge,** 1819, is an unusual design by Thomas Telford, its arch surmounted by a large stone circle above which runs the carriageway.

Along **Bannockburn Road**, the new **High School,** by Central Region architects department, is a curving orange-brick cliff with a cascade of glass facing north, almost certainly on the exact site of the battle.

HERE NO SCOT can pass uninterested wrote Burns in 1787. *I fancy to myself I see my gallant countrymen coming over the hill and down on the plunderers of their country, the murderers of their fathers, noble revenge and just hate glowing in every vein. . . . Four years later he was riding with John Syme to Gatehouse of Fleet. I took him,* wrote Syme, *by the moor road . . . the sky was sympathetic with the wretchedness of the soil; it became lowering and dark. The hollow winds sighed; the lightnings gleamed; the thunder rolled. The poet . . . spoke not a word. What do you think he was about? He was charging the English army along with Bruce at Bannockburn . . . Next day he produced for me the following Address of Bruce to his troops:* Scots wha hae.

Right: Bannockburn High School. **Below:** the Bannockburn Heritage Centre.

66 **Borestone and Bannockburn Memorial**
The Borestone, remains of which are embedded in the top of a granite monument, in a circular, concrete-walled rotunda, is overlooked by the splendid bronze statue of Robert Bruce, by C. d'O. Pilkington Jackson, a survivor of the Lorimer era whose dream it had been for many years.

The view to Stirling Castle indicates the commanding nature of the site, astride the main road to Stirling. It is now thought that the preliminary skirmish between King Robert and de Bohun may have occurred by the Borestone, but that the main battle of the following day took place along the Bannock Burn to the north east, where there is a much more vivid sensation of the steepness of the Bannock Burn's course through the marshes at the bottom which proved

so fateful for Edward II's army of 30,000 expert, trained troops summoned from all over Europe.

The National Trust for Scotland's new **Bannockburn Centre**, is a white harled block with rotunda, designed by Wheeler and Sproson. The **Hollybank Inn**, high on its hill, presenting a black and white face with Victorian finialled dormer windows, may be disguising an older structure behind. A two-storey gazebo adjoins. **Borestone Place** is very well worth a detour with c. 1900 Arts and Crafts houses in both Scots and English styles.

67 **Bannockburn House**, 1674.
The north facade encapsulates many striking features of Scots 17th century architecture: a main block, entered through a central, pedimented door (now protuberantly be-porched), with a roofline of decorative dormerheads, the ensemble flanked by the crow-stepped gables of the two projecting wings. Apart from the hall and later library, the finest rooms are on the first floor, the former drawing room (now the gallery of the ground floor hall) containing a huge, heavily plastered, ornamental ceiling not unlike those at Holyrood House, Thirlestane or Balcaskie by the Dutch plasterers imported by Sir William Bruce. Another (more restrained) version decorates the south east room on the same floor. Several rooms have good original interiors.

Originally built by the Rollo family, Bannockburn passed into the hands of the Paterson family whose Jacobite sympathies led to both the forfeiture of the baronetcy after 1715, and to their invitation to Bonnie Prince Charlie to stay in the house during the '45. The nearby ruinous doocot, 1698, is very tall and large, and the fine pyramid gatepiers are probably coeval.

Whins of Milton
Ruins of Milton Farm, possibly early 18th century, can be seen in the Bannockburn purlieues; traditionally the site of the murder of James III by a rebel dressed as a priest after the ill-fated battle of Sauchieburn. **Mill House** is the conversion of an early 19th century, stone-arched mill, whilst the nearby farmhouse has elegant neo-Tudor hood moulds and other details. The **Pirnhall Inn**, late 18th century, records a now defunct trade of making pirns or reels for the weavers. Nearby **Chartershall**, with its 1747 bridge, was a nail-making community.

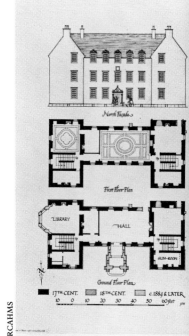

RCAHMS

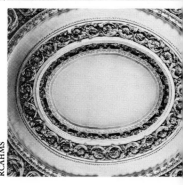

RCAHMS

Top: plan and elevation of Bannockburn House.
Above: the ceiling of the Hall with its late 17th century Dutch plasterwork.

69 **Old (or Little) Sauchie**, 1541.

A long roofless L-shaped tower, built by James Erskine, joined to a later 17th and 18th century wing, recently restored as the head office of Tilhill Forestry (Scotland) Ltd. The barrel-vaulted ground floor of the old building contains kitchens and cellars, and a wide, squared stair leads to the main, well-lit hall which occupies most of the building. A corbelled stair tower leads to further apartments. The walls are remarkably well preserved, complete to their crow-step gables, and thoroughly defended by gunloops. Decorative *fleur-de-lis* wall plates have been added to the structure together. Private.

In the grounds of nearby Sauchieburn stands one of the finest surviving 17th century necromantic sundials rescued from Barnton House in Edinburgh. Dated 1630 and 1692 it consists of a pyramidical pinnacle sitting on a polyhedron, which itself caps a square shaft incised with various dials.

70 **Howietoun Fish Farm**, 1874-78

Sir James Maitland's pioneering, experimental, scientific fish farm became internationally celebrated. As the Historic Buildings Council has it *he was to fish farming what Turnip Townsend was to agriculture.* Twelve graded ponds are linked by channels and wooden culverts to a single storey running house supported on octagonal brick piers decorated with fishy themes, and from which fish could be fed through a hatch. The farm of Lower Canglour, nearby, is though to have been the site of the Battle of Sauchieburn.

71 **Buckieburn Church**, 1750.

High on the moor, this church was the first to be built in the parish after St Ninians parish church itself five miles away in the Carse. It is a rectangular, harled church, with square headed windows and outside shutters, containing two mural paintings by William Crosbie within.

72 **Craigend**, 18th century.

An exquisite, symmetrical, white harled farmhouse — a single storey harled pavilion on the right and a two-storeyed circular staircase bow projecting from the rear.

73 **Auchenbowie House**, 1666.

Home of the Bruces of the Auchenbowie (whose earlier lodging survives yet in Stirling), it began life as an anachronistic, tall, narrow L-shaped

Top: Old Sauchie.
Above: Howietoun Fish Farm.

building, the principal, carved doorway in an octagonal staircase in the re-entrant. It was extended both in 1768 and in the 19th century, and its internal details include excellent fireplaces and plasterwork of the Adam type. The garden contains a fine 1702 sundial with a plinth of panelled and incised stones.

74 **Common Hill**, by West Plean, is an early iron-age *homestead* consisting of a circular encampment enclosed by a ditch which used to enclose a circular timber farmhouse and barn with other out-buildings. The adjacent 18th/19th century farmhouse, on a rise above a burn, is cream harled with red windows, in mock Tudor style, with massed chimneys, gables, and gabled porch. The adjacent steading is a large stone built courtyard, the entrance surmounted by a bellcote.

75 **Plean House**, 1820.
A ruined two-storey classical house with a Doric porch and pilasters. The adjacent walled garden and pedimented stable courtyard are in a neglected state.

Plean is generally unspectacular, a mainly inter-war coal mining village. Note the grand stone 1874 school; the parish church with corbelled bellcote; and some spacious stone cottages at the eastern end of the Falkirk Road.
William Simpson's Home, 1833, by William Stirling, in cottage style notable for its shafted chimneys, was built as a home for *decayed soldiers and sailors*, with money left by the East Indian trader Francis Simpson. It was inflated by Wardrop and Reid in 1872.

Top: Auchenbowie House.
Above: Sundial at Sauchieburn.

E

RCAHMS

76 Plean Tower, after 1449.
Starkly visible from both motorway and railway, Plean Tower (or Mengie Castle) was built by Thomas Somerville with whose family it stayed for 200 years before passing to the Nicolsons of Carnock. Its caphouse was discourteously replaced by an orielled top floor in the early 20th century: but is now roofless. A straight stairway led directly to a first floor hall (the ground possibly being vaulted), with a window with stone seats, and a large fireplace with carved columns. The west flank of a 16th century vaulted courtyard range survives.

RCAHMS

77 Bruce's Castle, originally the Tower of Carnock, is a ruined fragment of a larger, early 15th century rectangular tower possibly built by Somerville's father-in-law, Sir William de Airth de Plean. It passed to the Bruces of Auchenbowie, and, after the construction of the beautiful, but now demolished, Carnock House later in that century, became known as Bruce's Castle to distinguish it from the mansion.

RCAHMS

78 Stewarthall (now demolished), 16th-17th century.
A sad loss. An ancient, unpretentious, home of great charm in the flat, remote lands of the Forth estuary, both architecture and setting seeming more French than Scots. Essentially a small towerhouse, extended in the 17th century into a broad mansion block one room deep; presumably undertaken by Archibald Stirling in 1702 subsequent to his marriage to Anna Hamilton, from which dated the beautifully carved armorial panels.

NORTH ACROSS THE FORTH

RCAHMS

OPPOSITE top: Plean Tower, **middle:** now demolished Carnock House, **bottom:** the demolished Stewarthall.

Left: Cambuskenneth campanile.
Below: Cambuskenneth west doorway.

79 Cambuskenneth Abbey

A footbridge, formerly a ferry, links the Shore to Cambuskenneth (one of Scotland's most important abbeys) of which only the **Campanile**, 1300, and the west doorway survive. It is one of Scotland's greatest early gothic belltowers, (although restored by William Mackison in 1864), a dramatic, three storey tower in beautiful stonework, with a vaulted ground floor 60' high, and pairs of later double pointed windows on each face of the belltower at the belfry stage.

Founded in 1147 by David 1 the Abbey grew to immense wealth and considerable importance, with a similar relationship to the Royal Castle of Stirling as Holyrood Abbey had had to that of Edinburgh. In some old charters, its abbots were described as Abbots of Stirling. It was in Cambuskenneth that the nobility and clergy of Scotland swore fealty to David Bruce as the heir of King Robert in 1326 at the first Parliament to include representatives of the Burghs; and it was here, also, that, in 1488, James III was buried after the Battle of Sauchieburn. Of its many famous abbots, the most notable was Patrick Pantar, who became both Abbot and Secretary to James V.

At some point before 1562 the Erskine governor of Stirling Castle seems to have become the proprietor of the lands, for in that year the Queen confirmed the grant of a large portion of the monastery lands and the abbey to his nephew Adam Erskine, who was later to become Earl of Mar.

JOHN KNOX attacked Erskine for taking Cambuskenneth and its lands without shouldering the duty of supporting ministers, the school, or the poor as was originally suggested. Knox wrote that the reason why he did not was *first, he has a very Jesabel to his wife; and second if the poor, the school and a minister of the kirk had their own, his kitchen would want two parts and more of that which he unjustly now possesses.*

RCAHMS

Below: the Wallace Monument overlooking Causewayhead.

From the estate of Alexander Erskine of Alva, Mar's great nephew, Stirling Town Council purchased the site in 1709 for the support of Cowane's Hospital. To judge from the engraving by Slezer, very little was left of the abbey, since when the ruins and the adjacent village have slumbered amidst their fertile orchards.

The village, consisting principally of two streets, was originally inhabited mainly by salmon fishers, although it acquired a reputation for fruit growing, and carried out a considerable trade in shawl and tartan weaving in the 19th century. Few of the cottages can be dated with any confidence to earlier than the opening of the 19th century. They present a picturesque variety of one and two storey houses, some harled, some painted and some stone, many with the margins of the windows and the doors painted in traditional fashion.

Causewayhead

The immense volume of water pouring into the Forth, and its attendant marsh, moss and bog meant that for centuries, secure and dry ground was not reached until the other side of the valley. Causewayhead therefore derived its name from being at the top of the *Lang Calsey* leading from the bridge to the Abbey Craig. The maintenance of the calsey was the duty of the Town Council, which still preserves records of the necessity of having to repair this great stone road at various intervals.

80   **Easter Cornton** is a pleasant farmhouse, probably dating from the 18th century.

The Orchard, Cornton, c. 1900 is an unusually interesting house with windows and porch details not unlike many by James Salmon.

81 **22-24 Airthrey Road** are early 19th century stucco buildings of some quality.

The district between Causewayhead and

McKean

Airthrey Road was developed between the wars. A number of interesting single storey cottages with white harled, square pedimented fronts are in Cleuch and Ochil Roads, whilst an excellent pair of 1930's semi-detached houses can be found in Dunster Road.

82 Wallace Monument, Abbey Craig.
J. T. Rochead 1859-69.
The National Wallace Monument stated the organisers *will embody an idea as old as the first formation of society — that the highest exercise of human virtue should be commemorated by the highest exercise of human art.* The monument to Wallace was erected by public subscription on the initiative of the Rev. Dr Charles Rogers. It consists of a 220 foot high tower rising from a courtyard, in the manner of an old Scots keep. The tower is a masterly exercise in perspective — tapering towards the top, the emphasis enhanced by the spiralling stone ropework which encases the projecting 246 step staircase, and the tiered stone crown. Corbelled above the main entrance is a fearsome bronze statue of Wallace by D. W. Stevenson. Each chamber in the tower is vaulted, and there is a collection of marble busts by Stevenson and a bronze by Pittendreich McGillvray. One of the finest views in Scotland may be obtained from the top. Attractions include audio-visual displays, a Hall of Heroes, adjacent nature trails and a shop.

At the eastern base of Abbey Craig is the former hamlet of **Craigmill**, once notorious for smuggling whisky. The artist Joseph Denovan Adam occupied the castle-like **Craigmill House** at the west end, using it as a celebrated art school 1887-96. **Abbey Craig Park**, Hillfoots Road, is a plain mid-victorian villa with a 1908 tower by John Allan.

83 Powis House, c. 1746.
On the ancient site of Powhouse this tall, almost square Georgian mansion is entered through a semi-circular Doric porch. Quoins and dressed stone emphasise its windows and corners, a string-course identifies the first floor on which are the best rooms, and there is an interesting courtyard range and sundial.

84 Gogar House, Mid-18th century.
A two storey, pink harled house of some charm, chimney stacks on each gable, once the home of the founder of the Stirling Boys' Club and Chief Scout 1913-29 Major F. M. Crum.

RIAS Library

RCAHMS

Top: the Wallace Monument — 1859 drawing by J. T. Rochead.
Above: Powis House.

85 Blairlogie

One of Scotland's most picturesque villages snuggled beneath the great cliff of Dumyat, Blairlogie, consists of a scatter of white harled, pantiled or grey slated houses of the 17th, 18th and 19th centuries, some bearing date stones. **Montana Cottage** is dated 1765, **Kirklea Cottage** 1758, whilst **Telford House**, early 19th century, is a grander stone house whose name derives from a legendary link with Thomas Telford which a glance at the architecture would tend to support. The remaining cottages, with crowstepped gables, pantiles, slates, and varieties of creeper around doors and windows, are unreasonably pretty.

Struan is a Victorian villa with Gothic window-shapes painted upon a continuous dormer window; **Ochil Neuk**, combines Victorian barge-boarding with a classical pilastered and fan-lit door; whilst **Blairlogie Park**, early 19th century, is purer classical.

Blairlogie Castle (or The Blair).
Alexander Spittal 1546.
A substantial, two-bay tower house extended in 1582 to form an L-shape, extended later again. As usual, cellars occupy the ground floor, and the hall the first. The dormer windows of the second storey project into the roof, one of whose *fleur-de-lis* carving is similar to those formerly in Stirling's Broad Street. An interesting, original timber balustrade survives on the stair landing at the top of the circular staircase in the south east angle. The initials on the dormer windows AS and EH stand for Alexander Spittal and Elizabeth Hay in whose family it remained till 1767.

86 Logie Old Church

The oldest of Logie's ecclesiastical monuments is the romantic relic of the old church and graveyard on the right bank of the Logie Burn, probably dating from 1684. An inscription reads *this manse was builded at the expenses of the heritours of Logie and of Mr A. L. Douglas minister there AD1698 — I and my house observe the Lord.*

Logie Parish Church, has an 1805 spire by William Stirling — a square, pedimented tower up to the wall head transformed above that into an octagonal belfry with round-headed windows. Above that, and separated from it by a cornice, rises an octagonal spire. The remainder of the church, McLuckie and Walter 1928, is an elegant whinstone box. **Blairlogie Church,**

McKean

R.C.A.H.M.S.

Top: Logie Village.
Above: the Blair (Castle) drawn by Drummond in 1849.

Left: Logie Old Kirk.
Above: new summer house in Logie Village by Duncan Stirling.
Below: Logie Parish Church.

RCAHMS

Swan

1761, dramatically enhanced by its rugged and scenic setting, is a plain, small, single chamber secessionist building, harled on the outside and distinguished by its three pairs of double windows and bellcote.

87 **Logie Villa** was the school, designed by William Stirling in the early 19th century, with hipped gables and Stirling's characteristic Tudor chimney stacks.

THE MINISTER OF LOGIE, between 1598 and 1609, was Alexander Hume, a considerable 16th century poet, whose most famous poem is *Of The Day Estivall*, which describes the poet's contemplation of the sights and sounds of a summer's day.

88 **University of Stirling**, Airthrey.
1967 onwards. Robert Matthew, Johnson-Marshall and Partners.

Founded 350 years after James VI promised to found a *free college* in Stirling, this splendid campus is focused on the loch, centrepiece of Airthrey Park and landscaped by a pupil of Capability Brown. The **MacRobert Centre** and adjacent teaching buildings are on a peninsular bluff, linked by a high-level footpath to the residences to the north, which are designed in parallel blocks stepping down the loch side. The **Pathfoot Building**, one of the earliest completed, lies to the west by the main entrance. The design concept is centred on the contrast between white rectangular shapes and the superb rolling landscape, between the parallel flat horizontals of Pathfoot, and the monumental chunkiness of the MacRobert. The University spent 1% of its construction budget on commissioning works by artists — an act of patronage well worth emulation elsewhere.

Three views of Stirling University.

RCAHMS

RCAHMS

89 **Airthrey Castle**, 1791, designed by Robert Adam in heavy castellated style, for the Haldane family who never occupied it, is a most unusual building. All principal rooms are on the entrance floor laid out in Adam fashion in a sequence of differently shaped spaces. The family sequence (nursery, bedroom, dressing room etc, interconnect on the left); whilst the public rooms — Library and Dining room do so on the right. Both wings meet at the apex of the semi-circle in the Drawing Room. The castellated style of Seton House is here, but marred by additions to the entrance by David Thomson. Thus only the south front retains Adam's original concept, dominated by its central tower.

Above left: Airthrey Castle as it is now.
Above: Robert Adam's original 1791 design.
Below: interior of the Principal's house.

The **Principal's House**, 1967, by Morris and Steedman, is a single-storey L-shaped courtyard house set high on a bluff. As a result, little more than the strip of window can be seen. Internally, it has the quality one expects of Morris and Steedman houses, the superb principal rooms occupying the heel of the L with panoramic views to the south.

Morris and Steedman

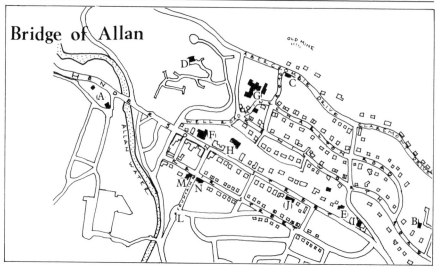

Bridge of Allan

ROBERT CHAMBERS patronised **Inverallan** thus in 1827: *a confusion of straw-roofed cottages and rich mossy trees; possessed of a bridge and a mill, together with kail-yards, beek-skeps, colleys, callants, old inns with entertainment for man and horse, carts with their poles pointing up to the skies, venerable dames in druggets knitting their stockings in the sun, and young ones in gingham and dimity tripping along with milk pails on their heads.*

McKean

Above: Inverallan House and the Old Mill.

Few people driving from Glasgow to Perth along the A9 realise the inflated extent of Bridge of Allan, for the main road simply presents a succession of desultory large buildings and hotels, joined by some pleasant villas and cottages. Yet, hidden on the south and up in the hills on the north are great victorian suburbs of which the main road represents but the tip of the iceberg.

Its origins are threefold: the original mill village of Inverallan; the ancient copper mines of Airthrey seemingly mined by the inhabitants of Pathfoot; and the development of the Henderson estate into a grand spa.

A Of Inverallan survives the **Old Mill**, 1710, a rubble built, L-plan, crowstepped building overwhelmed by its more modern neighbours, restored by Alex Strang Associates in 1979, and 18th century **Inverallan House** with its splendid doorway in the James Gibbs manner.

Uphill to the east, lay ancient copper mines in the Airthrey estate, closed in 1807 by Sir Robert Abercromby when he bought the estate from the Haldanes and emparked it, obliterating the
B village of Pathfoot: save for **East Lodge**, Logie Lane, a comfortable harled Laird's house of
C 1731. **Mine House**, 4 Mine Road, 1738, is another survivor of this era although somewhat Victorianised — a long plain white harled building in lovely grounds. Abercromby, however, had the waters passing through the mine analysed, and their healing qualities publicised. That led, inexorably, to the third stage: the development of the Henderson estate.

RCAHMS

The Hendersons lived at the west end in
D **Westerton House**, Alexander Drive, 1803,
probably by William Stirling. It is a fine regency
mansion with its shallow classical detail,
fanlight, wrought ironwork and Doric Porch.
When Major John Henderson succeeded to the
estate in 1844, the village consisted of *a few
plain whitewashed cottages by the bridge* — a trifle
exaggerated since **Henderson Street**, the
E principal thoroughfare, boasted the **Old Manor
Hotel** (no 129) which dates in part from 1766;
F and the large neo-Jacobean **Royal Hotel** was
begun in 1842. The cottages themselves,
opposite the Westerton Arms, were designed by
William Stirling in 1831.

The pressure for a spa could not be contained,
and, apart from the rash of new hotels on the
G main road, the focus was the **Allan Water
Hotel**, 1860-68 the rump of which still survives.
It was a rambling building in a combination of
towered Italianate and barge-boarded
romanesque designed by James Hamilton, and
the 1861 **Well House**, alongside, by William
Mackison, is gothic, Pumping machinery
survives 130' below.

Major Henderson took a personal interest in
the feuing, delighting, so it was said, in the
elegant walks and promenades. The buildings of
Henderson Street display the usual mixture of
rubble and well dressed chimneys. Specifically
H worthy of note is the **Chalmers Church**, 1856
by J. W. and J. H. Hay, a low slung building in
English mid-pointed style, its gracefully spired
south tower more cottage-like in scale than
I normal. The **Museum Hall**, 1886-7 by
E. Simpson is somewhat over-arcaded in a
marriage between a Wesleyan Chapel and a
J romanesque Venetian palazzo. **Belmoir House**,
no 118-24, by James Collie, 1851, is a two-storey
classical villa.

Top left: Westerton House.
Top: the Chalmers Church —
original drawing of 1856.
Middle: the Allan Water Hotel.
Bottom: the Museum Hall.

McKean

BY 1845 BRIDGE OF ALLAN had become a *favourite watering place . . . Here the visitor finds himself transported to a district of fertile and cultivated beauty — a country rich in verdant pastures sprinkled with the comfortable habitations of man, and awakening more of a home feeling in his bosom than nature in her free, wild, unadorned loveliness.*

Upper Bridge of Allan

Bridge of Allan is divided by Henderson Street into two quite distinct communities: uphill to the north, and downhill to the low-lying flood plain of the Allan Water. Roads such as Kenilworth Road, Chalton Road and Abercromby Drive — all watering holes near the spa — consist of large mid-Victorian mansions in spacious grounds, many stone walled. The architecture is similar to that in the King's Park of Stirling, save that it is more ruggedly baronial in keeping with its dramatic setting. In consequence, plenty of rubble, dressed stone surrounds to windows and doors, some ashlar fronts, dormer windows, carvings, mouldings, raised quoins on the corners, and pilasters flanking the doors.

Kenilworth Road

No 10 is identified by its Jacobean shaped gable dominating the entrance and **no 14** was alpine in style its facade consisting of a huge three-bay broad-eaved bargeboarded gable. **Coneyhill House** (26-28) has barged boarded gables, its gate piers dominated by sculptured eagles. The house beside **Glenisla** has Arts and Crafts details, hipped roofs, half timbered with a huge greenhouse. **Eastwell** (no 47) probably designed by William Mackison, is very Italian in style whereas **Wellpark**, next door, is in Dutch Jacobean in detail.

Chalton Road

A series of rather grander villas, each one its own little spa castle, most probably from the same architect, some of the details clearly plundered from the grander baronial mansions of David Bryce. **Rokeby** (no 33) and the similar double villa of **43-45** may stand as representing their best corbelled, crow-stepped gables, projecting bays and ball-finials.

Uplands, 15 Abercromby Drive, 1907, is a notable, large mansionhouse by William Leiper, in his English manner: part harled, part timbered, mullioned windows, oriel windows, a tower and a Tudor Porch. **Drumpark House**, 7 Claremount Drive, 1905, was built as a sanatorium by Charles Soutar, with swept roofs, gables and tapering chimney stacks: not so much Bridge of Allan as seaside architecture as befits a sanatorium: harled and whitewashed, tile hung, timber verandahs, and semi-circular windows in the attic. **4-6 Well Road**, 1840-50 is a throw-back classical villa, with Ionic columns flanking the doorway.

HBC

HBC

Downhill

L The **Fountain of Nineveh** set in the middle of a pleasant Victorian circus, is a cast iron device in the style of a fluted Roman Doric column erected in 1851 by Major Henderson to celebrate recent Babylonian excavations. The basin on top is surmounted by a pedestal of dolphins, crested M by a stork. The nearby **Manse**, 21 Fountain Road, 1857, is a Gothic Revival villa with arched porch and trefoil-headed windows. **Keir** N **Street** is dominated by **Holy Trinity**, 1860, in early medieval gothic, with notable furnishings by Charles Rennie Mackintosh in 1904 — a pulpit, communion table and chairs, an organ case and choir stalls. The oak organ screen is richly elaborate, strongly vertical, marrying perpendicular tracery with Mackintosh's own attenuated flower- and stem motifs. **St Saviour's**, 1857, is a red sandstone building with different coloured dressings, enlarged by Alexander Ross. Keir Street is largely early to mid-Victorian, a sedate, burgher's suburb compared to the soi-disant lairds with their romantic fantasies uphill.

Swan

Main column — opposite: top — baronial house in Kenilworth Road.
Far left: the Rowans, 24c Kenilworth Road, 1968, by Archie Ferguson.

Top: Drumpark House.
Middle: 14 Kenilworth Road.
Above: Fountain of Nineveh.

Lecropt

A parish now bisected by the motorway, dominated by the great estate of Keir. The **Church**, its large Perpendicular, pinnacled tower dominating the end of the motorway, was designed by William Stirling, 1826, very nearly reproducing David Hamilton's church at Larbert. Hamilton's and Stirling's drawings bear the same calligraphy: perhaps William Stirling II studied under Hamilton, for it was the fashion for apprentices to write in their master's hand at that date. The interior is of particular interest by virtue of its arched and ribbed ceiling, and the plaster vaulted Keir loft at one end. The **Manse** dates from about 1800, a good plain house with a pilastered and fanlight doorway. The **School**, also by William Stirling, is contemporary with the church.

McKean

Top: Lecropt Church.
Above: Keir House.

DURING THE 19th century, the *policies of Keir* were transformed according to the landscaping theory that attractions should be revealed only gradually. In consequence, there may be found tunnels, footbridges with panelled parapets, parterres, two walled gardens, a range of greenhouses with pediments, urns, pillars and statues, a Water Garden, a Topiary Yew House, rustic bridges, classical bridges, cascades, an ice house, water house, garden house, stud house and bathing house — the last incorporating relics from Dunblane Cathedral. Such extensive works, accompanied by a notable collection of trees, shrubs, rhododendrons and azaleas became famous and were visited by Frederic Chopin (1848) and by Disraeli.

RCAHMS

90 **Keir**
18th century onwards: David Hamilton, William Stirling II, Alfred Jenoure, Sir Rowand Anderson.

Ancestral seat of the Stirlings of Keir since the 15th century on a bluff looking across the Carse to Stirling. The current house began in the mid-18th century, some interiors of which survive. In 1820 Hamilton added the Drawing Room wing, and the beautiful, hard edged, **North** and **South Lodges** with their adjacent Doric gateways.

In 1845-51 Alfred Jenoure (who worked for virtually no other client in his life) replaced the pedimented front with a billowing four-storey bow, the top storey designed as a glass roofed, open loggia. The Jenoure scheme was completed by Stirling, who may have designed the 1849 **Tunnel**, and the **Cenotaph**. Sir Robert Rowand Anderson added the north west wing, the 1899 **West Terrace**, and the **Chapel**, with mosaics by Boris Anrep.

91 **Arnhall Castle**, 1617.
Formerly the seat of the Dow family who

married into their near neighbours the Stirlings, whose policies overran it. It consists of a ruined tower and enclosure, with the remains of a corbelled stair tower or turret.

Kippenross, c. 1770.

The old house, the seat of the Pearsons of Kippenross, was destroyed by fire in 1768, and although the Pearsons began its replacement, it was completed by the Stirlings of Kippendavie, a cadet branch of the Keir family, to whom the estate had been sold. It is an imposing classical building, with a slightly projecting pedimented central bay, entered up a balustraded stair and through an Ionic pedimented porch. A balustrade with urns runs right along the top of the house. The wing was added by William Stirling in 1809, and the ensemble enlarged by Rowand Anderson; and then, 90 years later, reduced again by the firm of Rowand Anderson Kininmonth and Paul. There is a fine walled garden dated 1703 and a pleasant 1830 sundial.

Old Kippenross is a 1768, red-harled conversion in the Gothic style, of the 1617 L-plan house, the ground floor vault of which is incorporated in the recent restoration by David Carr architects.

Top left and right: original drawing, and executed design of the Lodge Gates, Keir by David Hamilton.
Middle: Kippenross.
Above: Old Kippenross.

DUNBLANE

McKean

IN 1843, the Minister recorded a very great depression and want of employment . . . so little encouragement having been given to public improvements, Dunblane has been as neglected as a spot as any in Scotland. It contains 1,800 inhabitants, a great number of whom are extremely poor and some in the lowest degredation and wretchedness. Two years later, the principal street was still narrow, inconvenient and ill-kept. Many of the houses . . . old and mean, and the use of thatch as a covering . . . more frequent than in almost any town of this size that we can remember. Yet you see what you want to see. Only the following year Billings recorded a pleasant sequestered peaceful village . . . a transparent flowing stream, with luxuriously broken ground on either side, well kept gentlemen's houses peeping forth from banks of rich foliage — a few irregularly scattered ancient houses, all crowned by the broken walls and the grey tower of the cathedral.

After all that, Dunblane lived down to its reputation. Despite the advent of affluence in the later 19th century, Dunblane remains more a Cathedral village than a city — less urban than, for example, Brechin and most of its buildings humbler than even those of Linlithgow.

Top: Dunblane in 1672 drawn by Captain John Slezer.
Right: Dunblane from the Bridge showing the Cathedral on the skyline.

This City owes its existence to its Cathedral, and to its location as the sole crossing point of the Allan Water on the main north road from Glasgow to Perth.

It never seems to have been a particularly wealthy diocese. The earliest illustrations and descriptions are of a community which has been disembowelled. With the abandonment of the Cathedral and its officers, the houses of Deans, Canons, Bishops and others fell to ruin, and the income they brought to the town was diverted to new lay proprietors. The view of Dunblane, by Captain John Slezer in 1672, justifies Sir Robert Sibbald's contemporary description *a pleasant little town on the banks of the river Allan, where the ruins of the Bishops and regular Canons houses are to be seen.* Indeed, most of the town appears to be in ruins, and only two of the buildings appear to have any quality or size. The roofless archbishop's palace had great tall chimneys, large windows, and circular towers implying palatial rather than defensive characteristics, but virtually nothing survives today.

McKean

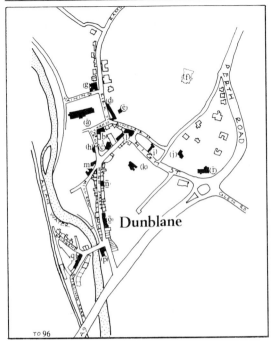

Dunblane

McKean

a **Dunblane Cathedral**

*He was no common man who designed that
Cathedral of Dunblane* wrote John Ruskin in
1853 *I know not anything so perfect in its
simplicity, and so beautiful, as far as it reaches, in
all the Gothic with which I am acquainted.* High
but well earned praise for a building smaller
than some English parish churches, and lacking
the architectural flourishes and cohesion of most
other Cathedrals; and one which only narrowly
survived the threat of demolition to make way
for the railway.

McKean

Left: Dunblane Cathedral.
Above: the west front in 1846
drawn by R. W. Billings.

DIRTY DUNBLANE wrote the
wordy Richard Francks as he
passed by in 1656, *let us pass by it.*
He clearly was expecting more than
he found. *I think it is but time lost
to survey the reliques of a ruinous
heap of stones that lean o'er the verge
of a river facing the mountains.* He
disliked the narrow streets, low,
little and dirty houses, dismissing
Dunblane as a *pitiful, piddling
corporation.*

F

Dunblane Cathedral nave.

RCAHMS

The Tower, late 11th century, offset, and slightly squint on the south, with romanesque arched windows in the lower storeys, the upper stage and parapet from c. 1500, bearing the arms of Bishop Chisholm, may originally have been freestanding. The **Nave**, c. 1240, possibly the finest part of the Cathedral, is eight bays long, tall and narrow, with aisles and a galleried clerestorey. Its principal attraction is its simple proportions, clustered shafts, and graceful clerestorey windows, in the west wall. It was never stone vaulted and, after four centuries of ruin, was restored by Sir Robert Rowand Anderson at the expense of the proprietor of Glassingal in 1889 with a timber roof not dissimilar to that of Glasgow Cathedral Choir. The **Nave** contains many items of interest: a pulpit, choir screen and memorial to the Keir family by Rowand Anderson; the 1271 effigies of Malise, Earl of Strathearn and his Countess; a freestanding Celtic Cross c. 800 bearing carvings of animals; the 15th century effigy to Bishop Ochiltree; and the six carved **Bishop's Stalls**, commissioned by Bishop James Chisholm some time after 1486. Robustly carved with animals, centaurs, flowers and leaves (including the Scots thistle), they retain their canopies and represent the finest Scots mediaeval woodwork (roofs excepted) outside King's College, Aberdeen. Within the buttress on the south side of the west door, reached from the south aisle, is a diminutive vaulted room now beautifully fitted out as **St Clement's Chapel.**

The Choir, in constant use as the parish church was never really ruined (save perhaps by James Gillespie Graham 1817-19 who removed its original tracery). Dating from the later 13th century, it is a tall, aisleless rectangle whose east gable and south wall are almost entirely windows; the absence of which on the north wall is accounted for by the existence of an earlier, two-storey building set against it. During the restoration, Rowand Anderson found traces of a triforium arcade, and indications that the upper storey was used as a chapel. The beautifully vaulted lower storey, often called the Lady Chapel, was probably used as a Chapter house. Sir Robert Lorimer designed the stalls, organ-case and screen in 1912. 15th century Ochiltree miserere stalls flank the Communion Table, and the sepulchural effigy in the north wall niche is almost certainly that of the founder Bishop Clement. The tracery of the fine windows is Anderson's.

The exterior of the Cathedral is, with the exception of the west front and the tower, simply an expression of its interior. The west front, squeezed between two hefty, asymmetrical buttresses is the composition so admired by John Ruskin and consists of three stages tapering toward a slender apex. The thickened ground floor is given over to the magnificent west door and its flanking pointed arches (a similar treatment to Inchmahome: see p 113). The three windows above — six times more slender being over double the height — are simple twin-light windows with a quatrefoil at the head; capped — at the apex by the oval window or vesica with carved leaves *made famous* as Rowand Anderson noted, *by a poetical but most inaccurate description of it by Ruskin.* It is a peculiarity of this Cathedral that its principal processional doorway faces the riverside, thus making impossible the grand views and aspect of the west front normally available in others.

RCAHMS

McKean

Top: the 15th century carved Choir Stalls.
Above: Dunblane Cathedral with the Leighton Library on the left.

83

McKean

The main street of Dunblane from the Cathedral. On the left is the Cathedral Museum, and on the right the Leighton Library.

b **Cathedral Museum**, the Cross, 17th century. A plain, tall, harled building with a forestair and later date panel and window of 1765, it sports the arms of James Pearson, first of Kippenross, who was Dean in 1624. Entered through a barrel-vaulted ground floor, its various changes of level are indicative of changing fortunes — including a later staircase. It is a treasure trove inside, including carvings, parts of old buildings, paintings and engravings of old Dunblane and four superb scrapbooks regarding Dunblane's history compiled by a former Minister.

c Next door, the former **Sheriff Court House**, 1844, by William Stirling, was built on the site of the Strathallan Town House in a grand neo-Tudor style with mullioned windows, parapets and an arched porch. The site of the adjacent gaol is now a garden.

Cathedral Square
Two sides of the square consist of Kirk Street, the third being the Haining and the fourth, the river. Kirk Street consists for the main part, of douce stone or harled two storeyed houses of the late 18th/early 19th century. The entire eastern side, built against the steep rise of Holme Hill, on which was located the original **dun** of Dunblane, has been amalgamated into **Scottish**
d **Churches House**, the entrance block to which is thought — from its fanlit doorway and

cornice, — to have been the Leighton Manse. A
fireplace dated 1741 was discovered during the
reconstruction. The **Chapel**, behind, was
created from a pre-16th century cellar thought to
have been part of the Archdeacon's House.

Uphill to the south east runs narrow,
picturesque **Sinclair Street** with its group of
late 18th/early 19th century houses. To the
north east climbs Braeport which leads into the
splendid **Ramoyle** an undulating, narrow street
of excellent Scots Burgh architecture. To the
west lies the **Laighills**, the flood pain of the
Allan and site of Dunblane's short lived spa.
Ramoyle, Kirk Street and Sinclair Street all
encircle the historic Holme Hill, which the
architect William Stirling chose as the location
of his huge, towered neo-Tudor mansion,
Holmehill (now demolished).

The **Manse**, on the corner of Braeport is a
reconstruction by Honeyman, Jack and
Robertson skilfully re-using William Stirling's
original 1829 Gothic screen and coachhouse.

The Leighton Library, the Cross 1687.
A simple, two storey, harled, rectangular
building with a steeply sloping tiled roof and
crow-stepped gables. The plain, east, facade with
its forestair leading up to the moulded library
doorway is transformed by the magnificent, if
weathered, oval, carved stone armorial panel in
baroque style — with the inscription *Bibliotheca
Leightoniana* with a crowning mitre above. The
west facade has pleasant round-headed windows.
Currently under restoration by Honeyman, Jack
and Robertson.

High Street

The U-shaped High Street reserves its grander
houses for uphill, and commerce for downhill.
The most distinguished building (historically) is
Balhaldie House, c. 1695, the town house of
the Drummonds of Balhaldie in which
Drummond entertained Bonnie Prince Charlie in
September 1745. Little architectural detail
survives. **Woodend**, 1840, built for himself by
architect William Stirling II is a simple villa
whose rubble walls contrast with finely dressed
stone around doors and windows. **St Blane's
House**, 1835 and earlier, is an interesting
historical pot-pourri, part harled, part stone,
with a curious pedimented, Doric-columned
portico. **St Blane's Church**, 1843, a fine,
Gothic, disruption church closes the north vista
of the High Street. **Nos 89-95**, adjoining, are

McKean

RCAHMS

Top: the Manse.
Above: Scottish Churches House.

THE LEIGHTON LIBRARY was
built by James Robinson to the
commission of Edward Lightmaker,
brother-in-law to Bishop Robert
Leighton, to house the books the
Bishop left to the diocese in his
will. Leighton, Bishop from 1661
till his translation to Glasgow ten
years later, was preoccupied with
reconciling Presbyterian to
Episcopalian. Perceiving the forces
against reconciliation as too
powerful, he resigned stating *he
would not have Christianity itself,
much less a form of church
government, planted in a country at
such expense of blood.* The library
contains a remarkable collection of
theological, topographical, occult
and historical books, in a reading
room whose oak bookcases date
from 1840.

VICTORIA WINE (nos 58-62) is a good Italianate building of 1884 with cornice, architraves above the windows and flanking bays; in other words, a high quality mercantile building for the old established Stirlingshire/Perthshire firm D. & J. MacEwen which boasted *wines of every description, very old, in wood and in bottle, from the best shippers, Old Islay, Glenlivet, Burntisland and other whiskies, Prestonpans, Edinburgh and Alloa Table beer, Barclay, Perkins and Reid and Co's London Porter, and excellent dinner sherry . . . Feeding oats, Beans, India meal, Dog biscuit, Greaves etc.*

picturesque 18th century, harled houses, one with a rare, curving, forestair. **Bank House** (no 63), 1835, is distinguished by its pedimented doorway and original glazing (save in the dummy window required to balance the facade). **No 61** on the corner of Mill Row, has a pillared and pedimented doorpiece and a ball finial on the gable.

No 22-24, dated 1726, contains a near-invisible armorial panel, and its two neighbours (nos 16-20) are about 200 years old.

Facing both up the High Street and down Mill Row is the tall, early 19th century **Stirling Arms Hotel**, whose later oriel window, beautifully curvilinear wall head gable, and pedimented, pilastered doorway testify to its quality.

Dunblane Bridge, from 1409.
The ancient bridge links the High Street to Stirling Road and Bridgend — an equally historic part of Dunblane largely sacrificed to the railway. The original bridge was a single arched bridge of yellow dressed stone, built by Bishop Finlay Dermoch in 1409, relics of which may be seen from the north. It was widened to the south in 1849 in red stone, and pavements were added by the girder bridge superimposed in 1927. Stirling Bridge was luckier.

On the south side, the road splits. Bridgend, a steep, narrow, pavementless Scots street retains its pre-railway atmosphere as the ancient route to Doune. **Bernadette's**, corner of Bridgend, has a marriage lintol WM 1735 AH, and one of Queen Victoria's horse shoes nailed to the gable. The adjacent houses up to the **Railway Hotel** are also 18th century.

St Mary's Episcopal Church
John Henderson, 1844.
Small but elegant early Gothic buttressed box with bellcote.

Glen Road, leading down the Allan Valley to Bridge of Allan, is the main access to Sheriffmuir and the location of some interesting houses. **Tomdoran**, 1865, is a Jacobean mansion house with a gabled entrance bay and an arched doorway. **Glenacres**, also 1865, is more Gothic. **Kincairn**, 1905, is by Rowand Anderson. **Inverlochy**, 1947-50 by Alex Strang is a rare house from the period of building licensing. Its debt to the 1930s is clear from its projecting bay window and white harl tempered by the pitched roof and verandah of the Festival of Britain period. He built **Silverburn** for

Below: Inverlochy.
Bottom: Silverburn.

Strang

himself in 1967, a much purer vision of a floating pavilion set in beautifully landscaped grounds.

97 **Dunblane Hydro**
Peddie and Kinnear 1875-6.
Grand Italian palace on the hillside, the seven-storeyed tower dominating both the beautiful grounds and the surrounding locality. A whiff of late Victorian Mediterranean. **Ledcameroch**, next door, 1884, is more fantastic with its pyramid-roofed tower, but nothing like so stylish. **Anchorfield**, just up the main road, is part 18th century, harled and whitewashed with painted margins.

98 **Queen Victoria School, Dunblane**
John A. Campbell, 1907-8
A boarding school for the children of sevicemen, to commemorate both the recently deceased Queen Victoria, and those Scots servicemen who had been killed in the Boer War. The complex consists of the Boarding School 1908, the Memorial Chapel, a squat form clearly derived

Top: Dunblane Hydro.
Middle: Ledcameroch.
Above right: Queen Victoria main block.
Above: the Chapel.

87

ROBERT LOUIS STEVENSON visited Bridge of Allan often, when a child which he recalled: *I shall never forget some of the days at Bridge of Allan. They were one golden dream.* The second verse of his epistle to S. R. Crockett, written from the South Seas, is a perfect evocation of Sheriffmuir:

Grey recumbent tombs of the dead in desert places,
Standing stones on the vacant, wine-red moor,
Hills of sheep, and the homes of the silent vanquished races,
And winds, austere and pure.

Right: Glassingal.
Below: detail from the now demolished Glassingal House.

THE LAIRDS OF GLASSINGAL were long prominent in the district. About 1560 William Chisholm of Glassingal was partly responsible for the dilapidation of the see of Dunblane; in 1869 Thomas Smith of Glassingal endowed Stirling's Smith Institute and donated to it a large collection of paintings; and between 1889-93 Mrs Wallace of Glassingal paid for the restoration of the nave of Dunblane Cathedral.

RCAHMS

from St Monans (with added ivy), the Infirmary, the Headmaster's House, and the high stone enclosing wall with wrought iron double gates. The most distinctive buildings are Boarding School and the Chapel: the former being an enormous four storeyed block, with crow-stepped gables, projecting semi-circular tower, corbelled balcony above the main entrance, and grand entrance gateway.

99 **Kippendavie** (Ryland Lodge).
1820 onwards, probably William Stirling Seat of the Stirlings of Kippendavie (the largest landowners in the parish) of whom the most celebrated was John — the Chairman of the North British Railway Company and instigator of the Tay Railway Bridge. A charming, rambling, two-storeyed house, harled with painted margins and stone chimney stacks typical of Stirling. The porch has a datestone 1517.

HBC

100 **Glassingal**, mid-18th century.
A two storeyed laird's house with projecting wings and heavily pilastered doorpiece. Of the much grander 1864 **Glassingal House** by Pilkington and Bell only the Lodge, unfortunately, remains. Quite apart from its idiosyncratic and highly crafted gothic detail, Pilkington had demonstrated in Glassingal that he was the Gothic equivalent of Alexander (Greek) Thomson in the way that the stone structure of the window bays was carried clear of the glazing behind.

SHERIFFMUIR
Three buildings in the increasingly arboreal
101 wastes of Sheriffmuir are of note: **The Inn**, a plain two-storeyed house with porch; the 1915
102 **Macrae Memorial**, a rubble built pyramid with coat of arms commemorating Macraes fallen in battle; and **Stonehill** farmhouse — a grander earlier version of the inn, with stone chimneys and an arched doorway. White-harled,

McKean

Left: Sheriffmuir.
Below: Kilbryde Castle.
Bottom: Row.

103 towered **Cauldhame**, is a drovers' inn
castellated by the Victorians and, later, another
seat of the Stirlings of Kippendavie.

94 **Kilbryde Castle**, 17th and 19th centuries.
Seat of the Campbells of Aberuchill, prior to
which it had belonged to the Grahams and the
Earls of Menteith. The castle was a large L-plan
house with the hall in the long wing, cut into a
rocky promontory on the banks of the Ardoch,
with square, pyramid-roofed turrets; but repairs
and extensions in 1861 caused a wall to be
knocked out, with the subsequent collapse of
much of the old fabric. Architect Andrew Heiton
was summoned from Perth and baronialised the
lot in multi-coloured stonework with a huge,
round, frenchified turret *in harmony with the old
Scotch Baronial style of architecture*. The
95 **Kilbryde Chapel** by Torrance is an 1864
crowstepped memorial to the Campbells of
Aberuchill set in an ancient graveyard.

104 **Argaty**
Clearly a site of some age since the Gothic-
fronted stable block dates from c 1800, repaired
in 1840 at the same time as the construction of
the main part of the house; *Bryced* with a tower
and western wing c. 1860; and *Baronialised* by
Stewart and Paterson 1920-23. **Argaty Mill**,
105 1955 by W. H. Kininmonth, is an elegant neo-
Regency, grey painted, pedimented mansion.

106 **Row**, J. L. Fogo, 1862.
Two storey, L-shaped harled building with a
massive three-storey, keep-like tower, at the
corner. Idiosyncratic dormer windows. Adjacent
Hillside of Row is an early 19th century
farmhouse with U-plan steading and horsemill to
rear. Fogo was the architect to whom the Royal
and Ancient Clubhouse at St Andrews owes its
present appearance.

SHERIFFMUIR was the site of
the last great dynastic battle in
Scotland: between the faction out
of favour led by John, Earl of Mar,
and the rising faction led by the
Duke of Argyle. Mar was a
spectacularly bad military
commander who failed to exploit
his enormous numerical
superiority, and permitted Argyle
to hold him to a draw, giving rise
to the famous ballad:
There's some say that we wan
Some say that they wan,
Some say that nane wan at a' man;
But one thing I'm sure
That at Sherra-Muir
A battle there was that I saw, man;
And we ran, and they ran,
And they ran and we ran
But Florence ran fastest of a', man.

RCAHMS

HBC

DOUNE

RCAHMS

107 **Newton House,** mid-17th century.
Three storey and attic, red harled L-shaped
Laird's house, once the property of an
illegitimate branch of the Edmonstones of
Duntreath. The circular stair-tower is, as usual,
in the re-entrant, but the unusual feature of
Newton is the curved gable of one wing. The
ensemble, once beloved of Sir Walter Scott, with
its high crow-stepped gables and ruddy colour-
washed walls, is the epitome of a Scots building
of this period.

Inverardoch, 1858, by David Bryce and one
of his largest houses, was built to replace
Newton: Newton survives yet, with fragments of
the now demolished Inverardoch built into the
walls.

McKean

Doune Castle, from 1401.
Controlling the principal routes from the south
to the north and north west, Doune was built by
Robert Stewart, first Duke of Albany on a strong
promontary at the confluence of the rivers Teith
and Ardoch. The Ardoch also provided power
for the mills whose ruins can be seen on the
opposite bank.

Believed by the late Dr Douglas Simpson to be
*the highest achievement of perfected castellar
construction in Scotland*, Doune provides an
unequalled opportunity to study the built
consequences of feudal decay in the late Middle
Ages. It was a period when the Lord obtained
his soldiers by paying for them — in which case
they could be bought by others. At Doune, the
principal entrance is through a long arched
passage beneath the Duke's tower — a passage
which could be closed against rebels in the
courtyard as much as against intruders. The
tower above has its own defended entrance and
contains the fine Duke's Hall, with minstrel
gallery, solar above, and bedrooms above that.

The retainer's hall occupies the remainder of
the north side, set above vaulted cellars and
linked, through the buttery, to the service area
and stone vaulted kitchen areas, on the first floor
of a subsidiary keep. The scale is indicated by
the fact that the fireplace occupies the entire
width of the building, and requires its own
windows and drainage channel. The floors above
the kitchen provide the principal guest
apartments — which would be warmed by the
fire, but a safe distance away from the Lord.
The wall walk remains entire around the curtain-
wall, but it is uncertain how many of the
buildings — including the chapel — intended to
be built against it were actually completed. The
partial restoration of the main buildings was
undertaken in 1883 by Andrew Kerr.

i **Castlebank Cottage**, 18th/19th century, set
into the slope beneath the Castle with
magnificent views over the Teith is well built of
stone with an overhanging slate roof. **Castle
ii Farm** is red sandstone and crow-stepped gothic,
a somewhat protruberant late 19th century
building on the Ardoch floor plain just below
the picturesque 1735 hump backed **Old Bridge
of Ardoch**, and hemmed in by the wooded hill
of Newton House, behind.

McKean

Doune Castle gatehouse from the
interior.

AFTER MURDOCH, second
Duke of Albany, was executed with
his son and father-in-law in 1425,
Doune passed to the Crown, which
used it as a prison, a hunting seat,
and a dower-house for Scottish
Queens. James IV thought it and
the surrounding fields to be *maist
pleasant for our pastyme and verray
commodious for our dwelling in the
summer season.* It was blockaded
during the civil war in 1570, in
which year it returned to the
Stewart family who became Earls
of Moray in 1592. It has remained
in their hands ever since. The only
subsequent alarm was its use by
Jacobites commanded by
MacGregor of Glengyle as a prison
for Loyalists during the '45, some
of whom — including the Rev John
Home (author of the tragedy
Douglas) — escaped down a rope of
sheets.

RCAHMS

Doune

The village of Doune reported Garnett in 1800 *is in a very improving state and pleasantly situated. What has chiefly contributed to the increase and improvement of this place is the introduction of the cotton manufacture. An extensive work, called the Adelphi cotton mill, was erected a few years ago by some public spirited enterprising brothers, the Buchanans of Carston. This extensive work employs about 700 persons for whose accommodations all the ruinous houses of Doune have been repaired or rebuilt. A street of houses built on the south side of the Teith, with a convenient garden to each, is called the new town of Doune, chiefly inhabited by families employed at the cottonworks.*

The *new town* of Doune was Deanston and was clearly responsible for reviving Doune's fortunes. Until that time, Doune was a small town whose fame rested upon its manufacture of pistols which Thomas Cadell introduced in 1646 (a trade perpetuated in the town's coat of arms) and latterly, for its excellent slaters. The late 17th century pantiled, single storey stone workshop, recently restored by William Cadell behind **35 Main Street** may have been the building in which Cadell made his pistols.

Malt Barns, 75 Main Street, projects into the street forming a gateway to the burgh. It is an 1835 transformation of an earlier building into a Regency neo-Tudor picturesque composition in the manner of William Stirling comprising a harled twin-glable facing the street, sporting a beautiful oriel window, and capped by ranks of octagonal stone chimneys. The remainer of **Main Street** comprises mostly two and three storeys, symmetrical, stone or harled or painted houses and cottages, the majority dating from between 1770 and 1830. A good burgh street such as this demonstrates how, in very small details, the buildings form a homogeneous street, yet each displaying some detail different from its neighbour. Some have quoins, some squared stone margins, others fanlights or good doorcases, there being immense variety in how

Doune

Above: Doune — a late Victorian view from the Castle roof by George Washington Wilson.

the doors, windows, edges, gables, roofs, chimneys or dormer windows were designed and built.

Doune Market Cross, with 1-11 George Street in the left background with white harled towers.

iv **Kilmadock Parish Church**, 1822, by James Gillespie Graham, is red sandstone perpendicular, vigorous at ground level, but completely unconvincing at the top of the south tower which ends in four shortened decorative v battlements. **St Fillan and Alphonsus**, 1875, designed by J. L. Fogo, is a rather more scholarly revival of first pointed Gothic with slender shafted windows and buttresses.

The **Cross** is a small triangular space, a main road leaving at each apex, the buildings mostly early 19th century, with later Scots revival on vi the north. The **Market Cross**, 1620, consists of two sundials, a lion, and the arms of Campbell and Moray surmounting a tall octagonal shaft which stands on a plinth of six steps. **1-11** vii **George Street**, 1894, by T. MacLaren, is a maverick, Scots terrace with turrets, designed from London as a built embodiment of *home thoughts from abroad.* Crow-stepped gables, corbels, inset doors, turrets, craft panels, and similar idiosyncrasies produce a Scotland that should have been but never was.

George Street lead down to a bridge: plain, classical buildings on the left and at no 13, a converted **Wesleyan Chapel**, 1844. The conversion to a house of a chapel of this date, which was built with typically residential, classical features such as regular banks of windows a central doorway and a fanlight, seems viii only appropriate. The **Moray Institute**, 19th

century is enhanced by an Italianate roof whose deep eaves project over the facade and have to be supported on corbels. **Muir Hall**, 1922, designed like a gatehouse to an English manor, but using Scots motifs such as harling, corbelling and crow-steps, was supposed to be in keeping with Doune Castle. **Auchendoun**, Stirling Road, 1902-06 by Watson and Salmond, a stone and harled mansion capped with a later red roof has the irregular, ground-hugging plan favoured by Arts and Crafts architects, and a beautifully shaped, two storeyed bay window.

Balkerach Street leads west from the Cross with some of the Burgh's oldest buildings, such as the **Red Lion**, and no 16: but nos 31, 32, 33, 34, 41 and 43 all date from the last 20 years of the 18th century and form a fine group. The converted Kilmadock Church makes an odd looking house, and **Cairnryan**, down Bank Street, may enclose part of an early 18th century building.

The Bridge of Teith, built in 1535 at the expense of Robert Spittall, displays his coat of arms in an inscribed panel. **Bridgend of Teith**, 1902-3, by Sir Robert Lorimer is a simple asymmetric harled house with overhanging slate roofs and bay windows in the Arts and Crafts manner.

Deanston House

1820 extended by J. J. Burnet, 1881.
Home of the agricultural improver Smith of Deanston who *changed the face of the country and turned the wilderness into a garden.* Burnet added a gigantic semi-circular wing to the front and a five-storey tower with Italianate details within and without.

Deanston

18th century onwards.
A smaller version of New Lanark in even unlikelier surroundings: an industrial community in arcadia dominated by the overbearing **Old Spinning Mill**, 1830, formerly powered by four huge water wheels. The single storey weaving shed has 24 vaulted compartments on 12' high cast iron columns.

Deanston Cottages are mainly one and two storey stone buildings, numbers 1-11 being Germanic and dating from 1875, whilst those along **Teith Road** are early 19th century plain with dressed margins. **12-22 Teith Street** are, to judge by the details of quoins and dormer windows, slightly higher class, and **Deanston**

Top: Auchendoun.
Above: Deanston House.

94

RCAHMS

School is a late 19th century Jacobean building with mullions, gables, bellcote, bargeboarding and decorative arrow slit. The estate to the south west is late 1930's in style — white harled houses with horizontal metal window frames.

11 **Doune Lodge**, 1805.
A white pedimented house on a bluff above the Teith valley possibly designed by Alexander Laing, its gentility masking an older house to the rear. The house is a seat of the Earl of Moray continuing the link begun with Doune Castle. The estate sports an interesting lodge, a superb walled garden, and woodland along the Buchany Burn, including a shrub garden, banks of rhododendrons and azaleas, a rose garden and pinetum.

12   **Cambuswallace Stable Block**, 1809 by William Stirling, is a spectacular palace for horses, the south facade flanked by end pavilions and a pedimented centre surmounted by an octagonal steeple and leaded spire. The nearby
13 **Doune Motor Museum** exhibits designs of different types from Hispano Suizas to Alfa Romeos.

McKean

Top left: Deanston from the air.
Above: Doune Lodge.
Below: Cambuswallace stables.

McKean

THE **MacGregor Monument** commemorates the MacGregors, or Clan Albyn. The clan was put to fire and sword after the battle of Glen Fruin, much to the benefit of the Colquhouns (who had complained) and the Campbells (who expanded). By an act of the Privy Council dated 3rd April 1603, the name of MacGregor was expressly abolished, and those who had hitherto borne it were commanded to change it for other surnames, *the pain of death being denounced against those who should call themselves Gregor or MacGregor, the names of their fathers.* By a subsequent act of Council, 24th June 1613, death was denounced against *any person of the tribe formerly called MacGregor who should presume to assemble in greater numbers than four.* MacGregors had to take the name of other clans, such as the Drummonds, Murrays or Campbells. For a short time in the early 19th century Lanrick was known as *Clan Gregor Castle.*

A further story lies in the fact that Sir Euan Murray MacGregor sold Lanrick to William Jardine, MP. Jardine came from Dumfriesshire but was shipped by family and friends to the Far East to avoid scandal over his lusts. There he met James Matheson, of Achany; and the two established a partnership selling opium based in Canton. Both later became members of Parliament and the partnership grew into the international traders Jardine Matheson.

114 **Lanrick Castle,** an old house of the Haldanes, was castellated and turretted in 1791, the entrance hall and main staircase later Gothicised. *More magnificent than convenient* thought Ramsay of Ochtertyre in 1801. *Our entertainment was Asiatic. Vanity of vanities! How many things do I see in houses of Nabobs for which I have no desire nor indeed occasion. (Letters). Some fine classical interiors survive,* although house and grounds are neglected.

The stable block has a central tower with pyramid roof, and the policies contain a rustic vaulted grotto in the riverbank, kennels with a verandah made of tree trunks, the MacGregor monument consisting of a tree built in dressed stone capped by a Doric rotunda, two lodges, a gateway and their very own private (1875) bridge.

115 **Cambusmore,** 1800.
This plain, three-storey, stone laird's mansion set high in a bend of the Keltie Water incorporates parts of an older building. From John Buchanan of Cambusmore, Sir Walter Scott imbibed *much information about the old Highlanders, and at whose house I spend many merry days in my youth!* (Journal). Robert Baldie added the four storey arched and buttressed *porte-cochère,* and the harled and atticked west wind in 1880.

116 **The Gart,** from 1833, William Burn.
Originally a small L-plan baronial cottage, the Gart was transformed in 1900 into a grand whinstone mansion, towered and turreted, with keep and dormers somewhat in the manner of J. L. Fogo. It has beautiful grounds, and a splendid raised site looking over the Teith to the Trossachs. Now Gart House guesthouse.

McKean

There has always been some confusion whether Callander is the last highland or the first lowland village. To the lowland traveller — till the 19th century — the sight of Callander was tantamount to a warning that he was now entering *Injun Country*, as Thomas Graham implied in 1805: *In former times those parts of this district which were significantly beyond the Grampian range were rendered almost inaccessible by strong barriers of rocks . . . It was a border country almost totally sequestered from the world.* The old village, such as it was, clustered around the bridge at the junction of the two routes leading to the highlands — the eastern route to Stirling, and the southern route to Aberfoyle. Earthworks of its **castle** still survive on the south side in the grounds of the manse. Its expansion began after 1763, when the Commissioners for the forfeited Drummond Estate laid out the wide street and spacious Ancaster Square specifically for army pensioners. Thenceforward, lowland characteristics dominated the Highland landscape. By the 1790's Callander had a population of over 2,000 in well built slated houses, although in 1799 Sarah Murray found the standards of inn-keeping so primitive that her room had been stripped of its carpets which were needed to cover new hayricks from the rain.

OPPOSITE centre: Lanrick Castle, **far left:** the MacGregor Monument.

Above: the River Teith from central Callander.

THE PUBLICATION of the **Lady of the Lake** by Sir Walter Scott transformed the Trossachs into a hitherto unknown Eldorado of the noble savage. To reach it, travellers had to come through Callander. In 1818 Keats found it *vexatiously full of visitors*; whereas the following year the Poet Laureate, Robert Southey, criticised it for failing to live up to its new responsibilities: *a general want of cleanliness . . . the houses seem to have been whitewashed when they were built, and never since that time; they look the worse because the windows are not casements but in wooden frames, which when the painter broke them are seldom mended.* The population dropped by almost half between 1797 (2,000 souls) and 1836 (1,100), to that, according to Hans Christian Andersen, of *not much more than a hamlet.*

G

The historic heart of Callander lies at the bridge, and its neighbouring mound **Tom an Cheasaig**, the Mound of St Kessaig (or St Kessog) the patron saint of the village whose annual fair was in March. It is one of the most beautifully sited graveyards in Scotland, looking up the Teith to the hills beyond. Most of the surviving stones and the octagonal watchtower date from the 18th century and later. The **Bridge** over the Teith is a handsome, 1908 construction of red stone, so detailed with its pointed arches, cutwaters, string course and parapet as to appear almost mediaeval.

The older buildings of Callander lie south of the bridge along Lower Bridge Street. **Bridgend House Hotel**, a white building with patently fake 19th century black timber boarding may well date back to the 17th century. **Teithside House** is a (probably 18th century) formal black and white house of two storeys raised above a basement. The **MacLaren High School**, 1907, by Stewart and Paterson, is a quality baroque-style school in well-cut stone, a projecting, pedimented entrance beyond curved flanking walls and colonnade. The remainder of the houses in the street vary from the 18th and 19th centuries; no 17 having a notable Venetian-style doorway, whilst of the pair of stone semi-d's at the bottom, **Craggan** has touches of Greek Thomson in its pilasters, ironwork and splayed base.

Ancaster Square, 18th century, is the centre of the development laid out by the Commissioners of the forfeited Drummond estates, no 1 dated 1773, and no 24, 1789. The houses are two-storey, some stone, some harled, some with pends leading to yards behind. It is still possible to sense the original atmosphere in this large square of small houses — overshadowed as they are by high hills on all sides. **St Kessog's Church**, designed by Robert Baldie in 1883, is in the early Gothic style with the peculiarity of a central tower containing the main entrance and a spire that challenges the hills around.

Main Street is dominated by its hotels. The **Crown**, the oldest in the Main Street is 18th century in style, white with black-margined windows (with chamferred reveals) attic storey, and main door dominated by a sturdy, black painted entrance. The **Royal**, designed originally as the Commercial Bank by David Rhind in banker's classical, is held together by a top balustrade; the main doorway is rounded-

Top: Callander Bridge.
Above: St Kessog's Church.

headed and pilastered whilst the first floor is overblown — the windows flanked with brackets propping up architraves, an off-centre oriel window.

Top left: Main Street.
Above: detail.
Left: the Roman Camp Hotel.
Below: the Veterans Houses.

A SUNDIAL by the Teith footbridge is forged from the head of an Ionic capital and is enscribed in 18th century lettering:
I mark not the hours unless they are bright
I mark not the hours of darkness and night
My promise is solely to follow the sun
And point the course his chariot doth run

 The Ancaster Arms is soberly baronial, confining its fun to a stumpy corner tower. The **Roman Camp Hotel** at the eastern end but down on the riverside is a different matter. Spectacular wrought iron gates and a turreted lodge facing Main Street lead down an avenue of trees to a rambling, harled, towered and turreted building of great charm and indecipherable age, although parts could be almost 300 years old. Its appeal derives from an early 20th century remodelling by Lord Esher, secretary to George V and a celebrated book collector.

 Yet further east is a fine group of 1928 **Veterans Houses** by Stewart and Paterson — beautifully composed baronial crescent with conically-capped towers.

 South Church Street is dominated by the squat, red stone **St Bride's**, 1861 by Kennedy and Dalglish. Kennedy was a former assistant of Sir Charles Barry. The cottages opposite are picturesque late 18th century whereas **no 10** South Church Street is an unusual red sandstone building with *Art Nouveau* details.

THE TROSSACHS

RCAHMS

EVEN BEFORE Sir Walter Scott set three of his most popular works in this district, word had reached those in search of the sublime that they would find their epitome by Loch Katrine. In 1799 Sarah Murray was drawn to see the wonders of the Trossachs: *the awfulness, the sublimity and the solemnity of the scene is beyond, far beyond description of pen or pencil.* What a challenge to Scott — here he set the *Lady of the Lake*, *Waverley* and *Rob Roy* with such effect that all other subsequent commentators could only perceive the landscape through the eyes of Waverley, Bailie Nicol Jarvie, or James Fitz-James.

The effect of Scott's writings may be gauged from the novelist Maria Edgeworth's letter to him in June 1812: *The year before your **Lady of the Lake** was published the average number of carriages which passed the road near Loch Katrine was from 50 to 60. The year afterwards, 270 carriages brought people of taste to the ground.*

Kilmahog

The road to Kilmahog is lined with grander Victorian retirement houses, enhanced by the inevitable church by J., J. W., and W. H. Hay — St Andrews Episcopal. There was a castle at Leny, thought to have been in the ground of Trean House, replaced eventually in the 17th century by **Leny House** part of which survives behind David Bryce's 1846, towered baronial mansion. The house has an unusual 18th century V-shaped garden, and a superb 1630 sundial with obelisk, unfortunately much weathered.

The hamlet of **Kilmahog** occupies the riverbank below. The Ettrick Shepherd, James Hogg, visited it in 1803 about which he wrote to Walter Scott: *a paltry village . . . you may guess that I was glad at getting safely past this village, for its name signifies the burial place of Hogg.* He was misinformed; the name means the Chapel of St Chug. Of the new buildings by the dam that Hogg spotted, the **Woollen Mills** may represent a survivor, being an interesting group with a 14 foot diameter undershot waterwheel. An ancient graveyard, burial ground of the Buchanans, lies at the confluence of the two rivers Eas Gobhain, and Garbe Uisge, and contains the memorial to Dugald Buchanan, the Gaelic poet. On the same peninsula, **Bochastle** represents the remains of a Roman earthwork fort. 500' upon on **Dunmore**, are the remains of a native fort. Indian country indeed.

The Trossachs

The most confused piece of nature's workmanship that ever I saw wrote James Hogg to Scott: *consisting of a thousand little ragged eminences all overhung with bushes . . . on entering them, surely said I mentally, nature hath thrown these together in a rage.*

Above: Leny House.
Right: a Victorian vision of Loch Katrine.

McKean

100

McKean

The Trossachs Hotel — a romantic confection to suit the wild landscape.

SIR WALTER SCOTT'S perception of the Trossachs was probably formed by the following experience: *There were very considerable debts due by Stewart of Appin (chiefly to the Author's family) which were likely to be lost . . . if they could not be made available out of the farm of Invernenty . . . Such was the general impression that they were men capable of resisting the legal execution of warrant by very effectual means, no King's messenger would execute the summons without the support of a military force. An escort of a sergeant and six men was obtained from a highland regiment lying in Stirling; and the author (Sir Walter Scott) then a writer's apprentice, . . . was invested with the superintendence of the expedition, by direction to see that the messenger discharged his message fully, and that the gallant sergeant did not exceed his part by committing violence or plunder. And thus it happened, oddly enough, that the author first entered the romantic scenery of Loch Katrine . . . with a front and rear guard, and loaded arms.*

Landscape which for its rugged romance was internationally famous, presented a challenge to architects: whether to confront or to sympathise. The challenge came from an engineer, James Bateman, whose task was to tame nature, not respect it. Thus he chose a sternly classical form in which to clothe the 1856-59 **Loch Venachar Sluice House**: pedimented pavilions in roughly dressed stone.

The fancy came from G P. Kennedy whose 1849 **Trossachs Parish Church** is a gothic chapel on a romantic hillock, with bellcote and fish scale roof; and who lent a professional hand to that of Lord Willoughby d'Eresby (a name well worthy of Sir Walter) in the latter's design for the 1852 **Trossachs Hotel**. The hotel's dominant feature is the towers whose roofs are so etiolated that they are known as *candlesnuffers.*

Glengyle House, at the west end of Loch Katrine is an altered 18th century building, the birthplace of Rob Roy MacGregor and, for a long time, the heart of the proscribed clan. The burial place of the MacGregors of Glengyle is a simple stone enclosure.

The North
The road north goes through the pass of Leny, a scene, wrote Scott, *so romantic as to possess the highest charms for the traveller.* On the left is **St Bride's Chapel** a small remnant of little architectural distinction, but a fine setting and a good 1825 monument to James McKinlay.

Was it not remarkable, wrote Hogg to Scott: *that you and I should, each of us, have had Glen Gyle a party in a ballad in imitation of the ancients, and that before we had either seen or heard of each other? The poetical sound of the name, Sir.* MacGregor of Glengyle was the officer appointed to guard the Loyalist prisoners in Doune Castle during the '45. A contemporary described him as *a tall, handsome man (with) more of the ancient mien of the ancient heroes than our modern fine gentlemen are possessed of. Honest and disinterested to a proverb, extremely modest, brave and intrepid.*

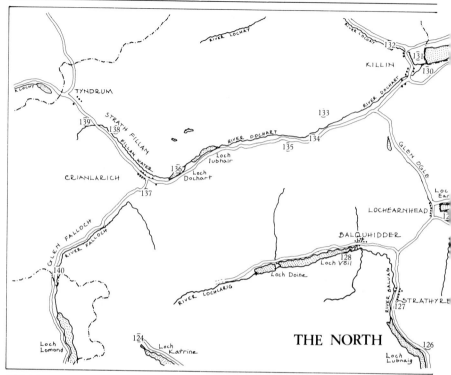

RIVER LOCHAY

RIVER LOCHAY

132

131

KILLIN

130

R. LOCHY

TYNDRUM

139

138

STRATH FILLAN

FILLAN WATER

RIVER DOCHART

133

134

135

136

Loch Iubhair

137

CRIANLARICH

Loch Dochart

RIVER DOCHART

GLEN OGLE

Loc Ear

LOCHEARNHEAD

GLEN FALLOCH

RIVER FALLOCH

BALQUHIDDER

128

Loch Voil

RIVER BALVAG

140

Loch Doine

STRATHYRE

127

RIVER LOCHLARIG

124

THE NORTH

126

Loch Lomond

Loch Katrine

Loch Lubnaig

OPPOSITE centre: Balquidder Church, **right**: Edinample Castle.

126 Facing over Loch Lubnaig is **Ardchullary Mhor**, 1910, a shooting lodge by Stewart and Patterson: really very good of its type: L-plan main block with crow-stepped gables, linked by rusticated arch to crow-stepped offices with projecting circular stair tower. It was here that James (Abyssinian) Bruce (1730-90) completed his account of **Travels to the Source of the Nile.**

Strathyre
Alexander Campbell, passing through in 1802 recorded: *everything in Strathyre is in character with the surrounding scenery, which is truly highland. The dress, air and language of the industrious and happy inmates of these huts; their rude implements of husbandry; the dwarfish appearance of their cattle; their peat stacks; in short, every article about their dwellings, characteristic of a people as yet but in the unpolished state of infant society. But, amid all this rudeness, to our no-small surprise, we fall in all at once with the newly erected village, the houses of which are built with stone and lime, and slated too!* Typical of the single-sided street of a highland community.

ROB ROY provided Wordsworth with the opportunity for one of his worst poems:

A famous man is Robin Hood,
The English ballad-singer's joy!
And Scotland has a thief as good,
An outlaw of as daring mood;
She has her brave Rob Roy!
Then clear the weeds from off his Grave
And let us chant a passing stave,
In honour of that Hero brave!
Heaven gave Rob Roy a dauntless heart
And wondrous length and strength of arm:
Nor craved he more to quell his foes,
Or keep his friends from harm.

27 **The Inn**, a dormered, harled building, is not unlike the military barracks of further west; highly suitable for this main military route from Stirling to Fort William. Of specific note is **Immervoulin**, a whitewashed courtyard of farmbuildings dating probably from about 1830.

Balquhidder

The heartland of Rob Roy MacGregor, who lived at the west end of Loch Voil, and is buried amongst a notable collection of gravestones (some very finely sculptured), in the churchyard by the **old parish church**. Now ruinous, only the east gable, with its bellcote, and the south wall surviving, the church is dated 1631, altered in 1774, when the nearby manse was built. The new **Parish Church**, 1853, is a bold gothic rectangle, possibly by David Bryce, built at the expense of David Carnegie of Stronvar. And some expense it was: the dressed stone was cut at Queensferry, crated, then transported to this **128** isolated spot. **Stronvar House** (now a youth hostel) is by the same architect, five years earlier. The nearby stables probably incorporate the original Glenbuckie House of 1828.

McKean

129 **Edinample Castle**, 16th century.
One of the seats of the Earl of Breadalbane, mentioned in the **Black Book of Taymouth**, Edinample is a white harled, Z-plan building whose roofs were sliced in 1790 when the interior was being classicised to high quality. It is now under restoration by Nicholas Groves-Raines. The adjacent 18th century mausoleum is a harled rectangle with quoins and gables, and the nearby bridge is contemporary.

THE SUICIDAL Paisley Weaver, Robert Tannahill, chose the Braes of Balquhidder for one of his most famous poems, adapted into a famous 20th century folk song:
Now the summer is in prime
Wi' the flowers richly blooming
An' the wild mountain thyme
A' the wild moorlands perfuming . . .
Will ye go lassie, go
To the braes of Balquhidder?
Where the blaeberries grow
'Mong the bonnie blooming heather.
There is an air of desolation about this place. It was one of the first straths to suffer depopulation. Campbell again: *the immigration to the mosses of Kincardine and Flanders was chiefly from this glen and other parts of Balquhidder. The population of consequence is greatly diminished. The stranger will naturally enquire why so many infatuated beings wandered from their home which in every respect, appears preferable to the dreary waste that they now labour to cultivate. He is answered when informed that there are upwards of 20,000 sheep, where half a century ago, one tenth of that number were not to be found. Formerly the lands were occupied by 50 tenants; now eight tacksmen have the whole in their hands, and have divided the hill and dale into sheepwalks.*

RCAHMS

Lochearnhead

A straggle of mainly white cottages, chalets and hotels catering for people attracted by the splendid scenery, the water sports on Loch Earn, or by hillwalking, Lochearnhead began life with the customary *good inn*, which survives in a Victorian courtyard formation. It expanded with the arrival of the railway, and has continued to do so after its departure. The **Marie Stuart Hotel**, is a romantic, towered confection of the Edwardian period. **Glenogle Tweeds**, forms an elegant semi-courtyard of single-storey, harled buildings with tapering chimneys. A new stone **boathouse** on the loch-side has a dramatic shape more redolent of Java than Scotland.

Glenogle

A more wild and truly barren tract is hardly to be met with in the highlands of Scotland. Through it, Major Caulfield (General Wade's successor) had to drive a military road in 1749 on his way to Crianlarich. Perhaps deterred by *nature in its convulsive throes* his road was hasty, and speedily condemned, being superseded by the present route in the early 19th century.

Killin

A strategic location commanding one of the principal routes from the Highlands to the Lowlands, the district was originally the territory of the MacNabs and the MacGregors. From the 15th century onwards, it fell prey to the imperialism of the Campbells, after Sir Colin Campbell purchased the lands of Auchmore, becoming the first laird of Glenorchy. The sixth Laird, also Sir Colin, claimed to have *conquessit the superiority of MacNab, his haill landis,* following MacNab's unwise mortgage of the majority of his territory to Campbell in 1553. His son, Sir Duncan (Black Duncan) built five castles, of which Finlarig, Loch Dochart and Edinample survive in this neighbourhood. Thereafter, the Campbells ruled supreme, the

Top right: Loch Earn in the 19th century.
Top: new boathouse.
Middle: the Marie Stuart Hotel.
Above: Killin.

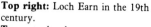

Breadalbane estate being second only to Inveraray in the Campbell hierarchy, its writ running from Loch Awe to Taymouth.

Killin is a very *long* village — a good mile in length — its southern end dominated by the roar of the spectacular **Falls of Dochart**, the irregular, winding bridge over which was begun in 1760. On the north bank is the **Old Mill**, 1840, a tall, narrow, yellow-harled building with mock-Gothic pointed windows and an overhanging roof — the house style of the Breadalbane estate in the 19th century. A padlocked gate from one of the bridge arches leads to the wooded island of Inchbuie, and the mainly 18th century **Clan MacNab Burial Place**, with its round, rubble piers and curving, arched screen wall. Out of sight, possibly on the site of a MacNab castle, is the walled enclosure, with ball finials, arched door, and a greatly weathered mediaeval grave slab. A private road leads north east to **Kinnell House**, the MacNab seat since 1580, although both Georgianised and Breadalbaned since. A long, harled building with well-cut stone surrounds to doors and windows, the house contains good 18th century interiors; and the policies a walled garden and a U-plan steading.

The growth in power of the Campbells, barely a few hundred yards to the north across the water in Finlarig (and one might note that within the same decade the MacNabs built a house, and the Campbells a castle) led to increasing pressure on the MacNabs. General Monk had to intervene during the Commonwealth to prevent *the molesting and intermeddling with the estates of any of the*

130

McKean

Above: the Old Mill, Falls of Dochart.
Below: Victorian romantic view of the Clan MacNab Burial Ground.

McKean

Killin Main Street.

KILLIN WAS once famous for its pearls. Faujas de Saint Fond, visiting it in 1784, recorded *though supposed to be a town, Killin is in fact only a hamlet, consisting of a few scattered houses at the end of Loch Tay. . . . I made a longer stay at Killin in order to obtain as much information as possible about the pearl fishery of the river which here falls into the lake. The master of the inn brought two fishermen whose particular employment was searching for the pearls. They led us to the river which runs in a clear strem over sand and pebbles, and they soon brought up several dozens of mussels, from about 3½ to 4 inches long . . . the shell is thick, and of a fine mother of pearl tint within, slightly tinged with a rose colour. There are some very fine pearls in the river mussels of Loch Tay, to judge from some which the fishers of Killin offered to sell us, at more than double the price of those which are in commerce. But these fine pearls are far from numerous.*

MacNabs who lived peacably. Their finances became parlous. Francis, the MacNab painted by Raeburn, attracted abounding legends concerning his attempts to evade creditors. A colony of MacNabs was established in Canada, and the estate passed to Breadalbane in the early 19th century, although Kinnell was recovered briefly by Archibald MacNab in recent years.

The Village consists primarily of the main street lined by the usual mixture of buildings — 18th and 19th century cottages, some grander Victorian and Edwardian houses, a craft shop in green wriggly tin inter-war gothic, and some very pleasant modern houses uphill to the west.

The **Parish Church**, 1744, was designed by John Douglas (described by Edinburgh architect John Baxter as *a cub who could never work a piece of good work all his days,*) and built by the Jacobite mason Thomas Clark. Originally a white harled octagon more like a distillery than a church, it has been extended on two sides, one with a bellcote. The northern shore of Loch Tay used to be so densely populated that outdoor services were held in the graveyard behind and communion in relays inside the church. The population has mostly gone. St Fillan's Market used to be held every January in the space alongside, in front of the hotel.

131 **Finlarig Castle**, 16th century.
Securely sited on a peninsula between the Lochay and Loch Tay, Finlarig was a strong, Z-plan tower of which only one gable now survives to any height. According to the **Black**

McKean

RCAHMS

Book of Taymouth, Sir Duncan Campbell *biggit the castle of Finlarig, pit and office houses thereof; repaired the chapel thereof, and decored the same inwardly with pavement and painting; for the bigging and workmanship thereof he gave £10,000.* It included a beheading pit.

Beside the castle are the shattered remains of the **Breadalbane Mausoleum**, an 1829 tudor Chapel by William Atkinson, in stuccoed brickwork, probably on the site of a chapel and burial place erected about 1523 by Sir Colin Campbell. Old dormer windows from the castle are built into the Gothic gates to the mausoleum.

132 **Glen Lochay House**, 1855, is a splendid, L-plan, mansion in Breadalbane Gothic, that is to say picturesque barge-boarded gables and dormer windows.

BLACK DUNCAN was *ane great Justiciar all his time, through the which he sustained the deadly feud of the Clan Gregour ane long space. And besides that, he causit execute to the death mony notable lymmaris. He beheadit the Laird of McGregor himself at Kandmoir, in the presence of the Earl of Atholl, the Justice Clerk, and sundry other noblemen.*

HBC

Top left: Killin Church.
Above: Finlarig Castle drawn in 1833 by Janet Stewart of Ardwell.
Left: Glenlochay House.

133 **Auchlyne**, a classical house of 1760 with a pedimented, projecting centre bay, wooden porch, and bows on the flanks, has a contemporary walled garden, and a nearby ruined chapel with little surviving architectural 134 feature. **Luib Hotel** (now a farmhouse) has picturesque, steep pitched, barge-boarded gables and an earlier, two-storey wing. The **Old House** 135 **of Suie** is an 18th century laird's house with a pleasantly Victorianised south front. The nearby burial enclosure at Innishewan House is that of the MacNabs of Innishewan and dates from about 1758; with tombstones of 1766 onwards. 136 **Loch Dochart Castle**, a contemporary of Finlarig, occupies an entire island and from what little survives, it can be seen that the castle consisted of a large rectangular block with a circular tower at one end.

Crianlarich

Crianlarich is celebrated, not for its buildings which are but few, but for its railway station which used to provide — so it was said — the best railway platform breakfast obtainable in the United Kingdom. The tiny church is a rare 137 building by Dr Thomas Ross.

Strath Fillan

Associated with the early struggles and hiding of 138 King Robert Bruce, Strath Fillan was also famous for a pool with legendary powers. Nearby, at Kirkton, are the scanty remains of the mediaeval **St Fillan's Priory** — the lower part of the walls of a long, narrow building. The nearby, 18th century graveyard has some gravestones of interest. The former **Free** 139 **Church** was erected in 1829 as a chapel by the Society in Scotland Propagating Christian Knowledge, before being put to other uses after the Disruption.

Glen Falloch

A picturesque glen linking Loch Lomond to Crianlarich, dominated by the beautifully part wooded course of the River Falloch, and a few scanty, bleached, stumps representing a memory of the great Caledonian Forest. **Inverarnon** 140 **House Hotel** was probably the laird's house during the post '45 period, extended in 1825, and Breadalbaned in 1830, as was the adjacent steading.

Top: Luib Farmhouse.
Middle: Suie House.
Above: Loch Dochart Castle, measured by MacGibbon and Ross.

THE ROUTE WEST

Raploch

An ancient community, sheltering beneath the Castle Rock. Very little now survives of the old village. **The Back o' Hill Tavern** is a typical late Victorian pub on Drip Road. **St Mark's Parish Church**, 1956, is worth a second glance as a post-war oddity; and the council estate facing Drip Road, designed by E. S. Bell in 1920, has been beautifully restored to resemble Bell's original conception of little Scottish palaces, some with towers and turreted roofs.

141

Kildean

Reputedly the site of the original Stirling Bridge and the battle thereat. The **Kildean Cattle Market**, 1967, by Alex Strang and Partners, architects of the unusual filling station in front, has an adventurous interior of arched concrete ribs. **Kildean Mill**, 1697, is much restored, its most recent incarnation with slated roof and dark timberwork being very attractive. A double sluice, and the seating for two wheels survive.

142

McKean

McKean

Left: Craigforth House in the mid 19th century.
Above: the inter-war houses in Raploch in Scots style by Eric Bell.
Below: Kildean Cattle Market.

143 Craigforth House, 1675.

Probably constructed by John Callander soon after he acquired the property, the house was much enlarged later, and completely remodelled about 1830, (probably by William Stirling, since the details are very similar to those of Garden, (see p 141) spread thinner over a much larger facade). It was gutted in 1930, and has been restored by Bell-Ingram, as part of their modern complex for Scottish Amicable. It is a substantial three-storeyed white mansion with a cornice and prominent 1830 Doric porch. The principal rooms in the house, on the first floor, are emphasised by pediments and cornices alternating above the windows.

Alex Strang and Partners

BLAIR DRUMMOND

Above: Drip Bridge.

RCAHMS

144 **Old Drip Bridge**, 1790.
The site of an important mediaeval ford, this picturesque bridge, now used solely for pedestrians, replaced a highly profitable ferry. 206' long with five segmental arches, it is rendered elegant by its piers, cutwaters, and voussoirs. The 1820 **Tollhouse** has a projecting semi-octagonal front. Nearby farm cottages at **Hill of Drip** present pretty groups of 18th century two-storey, harled buildings with stone chimneys and a later bow window, whereas **East** 145 **Cambusdrenny** down on the banks of the Forth is a small classical farmhouse.

146 **Ochtertyre**, 1760's, with additions of the late Victorian period, was the home and the creation of John Ramsay of Ochtertyre, a celebrated diarist and correspondent whose journals run to ten volumes.

147 **Blair Drummond**
J. C. Walker, 1868-72.
A dramatic baronial replacement of Alexander McGill's 1715 mansion which was abandoned on grounds of unsuitability and damp. Best seen, perhaps, from the wildlife park, with a foregrounds of hippos, the house is a bold baronial composition built of snecked rubble, with good sculpture. Mainly three storey, it also has a fourth storey entrance tower — a reminiscence of Burn's unbuilt scheme for Fonthill of 20 years earlier. The interior was replaced without any loss of grandeur by James B. Dunn in the 1920's. Currently in use as a residential Camphill community.
    The policies of the estate contain items of interest: the 1835 stable block, baronialised with

A LITERARY HERMIT
Ochtertyre described himself *whose books and garden are his luxuries . . . whoever wishes to partake of my fruit must report to my hermitage . . . chiefly cherries and greens, gooseberries and strawberries, a sprinkling of plums, two or three score of apricots and peaches* (1801). Ramsay's letters illuminate the extent that the larger houses of Perthshire were all intermarried within a few families — the Stirlings, Erskines, Grahams, Buchanans and Haldanes, new arrivals including Murdochs, Abercrombies and Muschets. His daily round frequently took him to several of those houses including Gartur, Touch, Airth, Airthrey, Kippenross, Kippendavie, Blair Drummond, Argaty, Cambusmore, Lanrick, Meiklewood, Leckie and Cardross.

a clocktower by Walker in 1871; a T-plan rubble cottage with bellcote (1835); an early 19th century egg-shaped ice house; an octagonal storehouse near the stables (1800); and a fountainhead, in which the spring issues through a doorway surrounded with rustic masonry (18th century); the Tudor Gothic 1830 West Lodge; the Tudor 1859 North Lodge; the classical, octagonal east lodge (1800); an obelisque in the grounds built by Lord Kames in the late 18th century; and the **Mill of Torr**, part neo-Tudor of 1845-50, now very overgrown.

Blair Drummond was the 18th century residence of the *enlightened and patriotic* landlord Henry Home, Lord Kames. He was the first major proprietor in Carse to attempt to tackle the 6-12 foot deep moss which covered the majority of the area, hiding a fertile bed of clay beneath. Kames began the clearing in 1766 and adopted two methods. The first was to offer short leases to poor people from the poverty stricken highland community of Balquhidder, on condition that they worked to improve the property. Although much approved to begin with, commentators soon noted that the poor people of Balquhidder were given the option of working extremely hard using, sometimes, pioneering techniques to improve property for 12 years; after which they had nothing — no tenure, income nor house. Kames' other method was to wash the moss away, to which end he constructed an enormous wheel to raise water from the River Teith, at Mill of Torr, The moss was cut into various sections, and simply washed away down the Forth estuary. Kames' technique was adopted by other proprietors, and within a few decades, the majority of moss had been cleared to produce rich farmland.

Top: Blair Drummond from the Safari Park.
Above: the stables.

HENRY HOME, Lord Kames (1696-1792) was not simply a Law Lord. A considerable philosopher, he was a leading member of the Scottish enlightenment, his essays on the principals of **Morality and Natural Religion** (1751) being written to pose a different viewpoint from David Hume. When he retired from the bench, he took leave of his fellow law lords with the following endearment: *fair ye weel, ye bitches!*

McKean

148   South of the main road, **Blair Drummond School**, splendidly closing Robertson's Lane, is an 1850 new-Tudor, fairytale building with a central tower crowned by an octagonal spirelet the wings on either side are two storey with bay windows. The architects could well have been R. and R. Dickson.

149 **Kincardine Parish Church**, 1814-16. Richard Crichton.
A prominent crisp, neo-perpendicular-style church — very early indeed of its kind, set slightly on a rise by the entrance to Blair Drummond. A chancel was added in 1907 by Harold Tarbolton. There are some interesting monuments inside. The nearby single-storey schoolroom with its bellcote dates from 1855 and the adjacent, towered schoolhouse from 1857. **The Manse**, by William Stirling, facing across

Above: Blair Drummond school. **Below:** Kincardine Parish Church and Schoolhouse.

McKean

Thornhill Road, is a pretty, Italianate design with overhanging eaves: a grand late classical cottage. Kincardine graveyard is the site of the old parish church, and contains two burial enclosures, decorated with fine armorial panels, one dated 1699; the other, dated 1686 was the burial place of the Muschets of Burnbanke.

Coldoch Broch, a rare survival so close to central Scotland, is about 30 feet in diameter, the walls themselves over 15 feet thick — having galleries and wall chambers within. The exterior of the Broch stands to only a few feet in height, and is much overgrown.

Gartincaber House
17th century onwards.
The original house was a simple three storey L-plan, harled building with curiously sculptured tops to the dormer windows, altered in the late 18th century. In 1820, virtually another complete house in matching style with crow-stepped gables was added, and a tower in 1843. There are some interesting interiors. The stable block of 1825-30 is built around the courtyard with semi-eliptical arches.

The ruinous **Tower**, erected by William Murdoch in 1799, just before he scandalised his neighbours by marrying his housekeeper, is a two-storey Gothic octagon with a parapet. It was built, according to Drysdale *simply for the wide and beautiful view it commands on every side . . . visitors are made very welcome to the key.*

Thornhill
An exposed hillside village, at the centre of a farming community, formerly noted for the

THE REMAINS of the old buildings, especially in some places of the Carse, form a striking contrast to the neatness and convenience of houses erected in modern times wrote Forsyth in 1805. *The old ones were in general formed of clay, tempered with chopped straw. They were built upon a foundation of rough stone, and the timbers which supported the roof were carried down to the bottom of the clay wall. The best situation for the accommodation of the farm is generally chosen. Dwelling houses on many estates, are two storeys high and are usually covered with slate or tile.*
Many of the houses in the Carse are of brick, well-plastered and finished within. To encourage this process of improvement, a Tile Works was erected at Blair Drummond in 1831, tiles being issued free to the tenantry to encourage improvement.

Below: Thornhill: Blairhoyle Masonic Lodge on the left.

McKean

H

Top: Norrieston Church —
original drawing.
Above: Rednock Stables.

THE LAKE OF MENTEITH is
supposed to be the only large body
of water in Scotland called a lake
(the remainder being lochs). The
title *lake* is late Victorian, prior to
that being called the Loch of
Inchmahome.

number of its whisky stills and public houses, of
which the **Lyon and Unicorn**, in black and
white mock Tudor, seems to be one of the few
survivors. It is really the junction of two former
villages, Thornhill and Norrieston, of which
153 **Norrieston House** survives joined to
Heatherlea: early 19th century two-storey
buildings with painted stone margins.
Norrieston Church was built as a Free church
in 1844, in the early English style with a two-
storey tower on the south east. The principal
landmark in Thornhill is **Blair Hoyle Masonic
Lodge**, 1893, a white harled, and red painted
building with a tower similar to nearby
Blairhoyle doocot at one end, itself with a doocot
half way up. The overall impression is slightly
Germanic, and of the style of Rowand Anderson.
The **Main Street** is long, the houses mostly
being one or two storeys, some harled and some
in stone. Note particularly the late 18th century
no **37-39** and the **Crown Hotel**, distinguished
by an architrave above the doorway. At the
western end, a modern triangular, harled house,
sits well into the hillside.

154 **Lower Tarr Mill**, early 19th century.
Ruined two storey mill, the lower part of which
had a kiln, with a waterwheel on the outside of
the west flank. The nearby U-plan, pantiled
steading and farmhouse are reasonably affluent
buildings of the same date.

155 **Rednock House**
18th century onwards.
The original U-plan house is masked by the
1827 regency mansion designed by Robert
Brown, built of channelled stonework and
dignified by a Doric porch, reached up a flight
of steps guarded by cast iron eagles perched on
Doric columns. Brown also gave James Ramsay's
1797 stable block a classical facade: pediments
on each wing flanking a central archway which
is pedimented and topped with a domed
octagonal drum. About one mile to the north are
the ivy-clad ruins of 16th-century Rednock
Tower.

Port of Menteith
The heart of the ancient earldom of Menteith,
and of the powerful Graham Clan. Its peaceful
setting, in a shallow bowl between the Menteith
Hills to the north, and the Campsies to the
south, gives it an English air.
The **Parish Church**, 1876, designed by the

114

McKean

Glasgow architect John Honeyman is buttressed Gothic, with a stone pyramid on top. **The Mausoleum** to the Grahams of Gartmore, designed by William Stirling in 1817, is a stone pedimented rectangle set on a battered stone plinth. The former **Manse**, possibly very late 18th century, has a distinguished gateway — stone quatrefoil piers splendidly encased in 19th century filigree Gothic ironwork. The hotel dates from 1854.

Above: Port of Menteith.
Below: graveslab of Sir John Drummond, Inchmahome Priory.

157 Inchtalla Castle, Lake of Menteith

A small island, about 30 yards south west from Inchmahome, entirely occupied by the ruins of Inchtalla (meaning a tower) castle, the 16th/17th century seat of the Earls of Menteith. The buildings were arranged around a courtyard, the northern wing of which was the hall, with a fireplace in the wester gable. The principal bedrooms were in the floor above the hall. The south side of the courtyard was occupied by the kitchens.

156 Inchmahome Priory, Lake of Menteith

Founded in 1238 by Walter Comyn, Earl of Menteith, for the Augustinian Order on an island already dedicated to St Colmoc, the Priory Church was built soon afterwards. The nave had a north aisle, part of the splendid arcade to which still survives, and the east wall of the aisleless choir is dominated by a slender five-light window occupying almost the entire gable. The remains of a sacristy opens to the north. The finest part of the church however is the west front, (with a later tower on the north west corner) whose processional entrance, with its flanking, sharply pointed, blind arcades with trefoils and quatrofoils above, bears a striking resemblance to the western door of Dunblane Cathedral.

RCAHMS

INCHMAHOME

R.C.A.H.M.S.

Above: Inchmahome from the air.

In the choir may be found the graves of some of the most distinguished families of the neighbourhood, particularly the late 13th century effigy to Sir Walter Stewart, Earl of Menteith, and his wife Mary. There is also a legless effigy of a knight in armour — possibly that of Sir John de Menteith who died in the early 14th century, and an effigy, complete with angels and dragons, of Sir John Drummond who died in 1300. Virtually nothing remains of the cloister, but the two storey chapter house is almost complete as is the vaulted parlour beside. *Open to the public. Guidebook available.*

MUCH OF THE beauty of Inchmahome derives from its majestic trees, avenues, bushes and flowers. Although legend has it that these are the descendants of the Monks' gardens and orchards, in reality they are probably descendants from the pleasure grounds of the Earls of Menteith which always occupied a major part of the island. In 1815, the islands produced *gooseberries, plums, pears, apples, Spanish filberts.* The surviving trees are the Spanish chestnuts, sycamores, oaks, ash, hazel, elder and thorn.

158 **Lochend**, 1715.
Originally the dower house to Cardross, consisting principally of a long two storey block with steep, old fashioned roof. The architraved doorway is surmounted by a 1715 date panel.

159 **Brucehill**, late 18th century, is a two storey farmhouse with arched windows, and a central oval panel: the adjacent steading is U-plan entered through a fine stone archway surmounted by a bellcote. Nearby, **Dykehead**

160 **Cottage** consists of a late 18th century single storey octagonal building with a porch: originally a tollhouse (and clearly of that ilk) and later a library. In the Moss, near the enchantingly titled

161 Pendicles of Collymoon, **Gartur** is a two storey

courtyard of probably 18th century farm buildings, once the residence of the Grahams of Gartur.

162 **Cardross House**, 1598.

After the Reformation the Erskines of Cardross became the principal proprietors of the parish from the Priors of Inchmahome and built this substantial three storey, L-plan building, with a four storey tower, and a circular staircase tower projecting in the re-entrant. There were many alterations in the 18th century, wings were added in 1790, and entrance hall in 1820. Some fine 17th and 18th century plasterwork survives. The two storey quadrangular stable block is symmetrical early 19th century gothic, and there is a nearby graveyard with stones dating from 1767. **Cardross Bridge**, 1774, was built by the government from the revenues of forfeited lands: it is 200 feet long, with three arches and cutwaters.

Above: West doorway of Inchmahome Priory, measured 1880 by T. N. Scott.
Left: Cardross House.

163 **Malling Mill**, from 1671.

A long, rectangular, rubble built mill, the wheel against the west wall. It is a particularly fine example of an historic mill, currently converted into a house.

GARTMORE

McKean

McKean

Top: Gartmore in 1900.
Above: Gartmore House.

ROBERT BONTINE
CUNNINGHAME GRAHAME,
the last Grahame owner of
Gartmore, became the first
President of the Scottish National
Party, although he had been
Liberal MP for North West
Lanarkshire 40 years before. The
family claimed, through the unused
title of Earls of Menteith, to be the
legitimate heirs of King Robert II.
Cunningham Grahame spent many
years in South America earning the
sobriquet Don Roberto, prior to
returning to Gartmore upon the
death of his father.

Gartmore

Exposed, picturesque hillside community on the
western edge of the Carse of Forth with
staggering views down it. The **Church**, 1790, is
a rectangular box with usual bellcote and porch,
reconstructed in the Gothic manner in 1872 with
wrought iron quatrefoils and finials. Closing the
vista down the main street is the somewhat ham
fisted 1790 semi-circular arched gateway to
Gartmore House, re-inventing 17th century
details.

164 Gartmore House
Early 18th century — enlarged 1779-80
Originally U-plan, Gartmore was vastly enlarged
by John Baxter, 1779-80, the east facade being
provided with two projecting semi-octagonal
bays. The remainder of the house was remodelled by David Barclay, 1901-2, after Sir
Charles Cayzer had purchased the estate from
Robert Bontine Cunningham Grahame whose
family seat it had been. To Barclay belongs the
idiosyncratic west (entrance) front, the tower, the
French roofs, and the weak Jacobean interior.

165   Not far to the north is **Gartartan Castle**, the
predecessor to Gartmore House — now a 16th
century ruin of possibly a Z-plan tower, little of
which survives save the lower storeys and the
base of a corbelled stairtower. Gartartan Lodge
is a small baronial effort, 1902, also by Barclay;
and Gartmore's walled garden, 18th century, was
clearly built with stone plundered from
Gartartan Castle.

McKean

Aberfoyle

Before the expansion of Aberfoyle in the mid 19th century, it consisted purely of a village or clachan, clustered by the Inn and the bridge. Sir Walter Scott's description of the village in *Rob Roy* in the early 18th century was probably founded upon interviews with surviving inhabitants: *the miserable little bourocks as the Bailie termed them, of which about a dozen formed the village called the Clachan of Aberfoyle, were composed of loose stones, cemented by clay instead of mortar, and thatched by turfs, laid rudely upon the rafters formed of native and unhewn birches and oaks from the woods around. From all we could see, (the inn at which they had stayed the previous night), miserable as were the quarters it afforded, was still by far the best (house) in the hamlet.*

By 1829, however, it afforded a *very comfortable little inn*, erected by the Duke of Montrose — the only landowner in the entire parish — who began a programme of improvements to his properties as noted by the minister in 1841: *the farm buildings are new and harmonious, and very superior to those generally found in the highland estates.* The ruined, rubble walls of the **Old Parish Church**, 1774, across the contemporary hump-backed bridge to the south, still survive with its bellcote on the east wall, in an 18th century graveyard. It was superseded by the **New Parish Church** and adjacent school, designed 1869-70 by John

Top: Aberfoyle from the Old Kirk.
Above: the Covenanters Hotel.

IN 1671 the Earl of Airth stopped Thomas Grahame of Duchray at Aberfoyle Bridge on his way to baptise his child at the Old Kirk. The baby was placed on the ground, both parties presented swords, guns and pistols, and the Earl got off with his life with great difficulty. Grahame of Duchray ended up in the Edinburgh Tolbooth.

Honeyman in the approved Gothic style. **St Mary's Episcopal Church**, 1893-4 by James Miller is rather more highland — harled with red stone dressings, and a bellcote. Craighuchty Terrace, 1895 also by Miller, is a confident row of six large houses whose ground floor is built of red stone and the first floor is tile hung with half timbering in the English style.

166 **Duchray Castle**
16th century
The seat of the Grahames of Duchray and Rednock comprises a rectangular block with attached round tower with a conical turret. It was later extended and, in 1845, fitted up as a hunting lodge. The mock Gothic windows may have been intruded into the old building at that time.

RCAHMS

McKean

167 **David Marshall Lodge**, 1958, James Shearer, is a single storey rubble building with a concrete portico, with wings radiating from the centre above which there is a tower with a

168 pyramid roof. **Milton Mill**, 1667, is a picturesque but derelict building retaining its 14

169 foot cast iron wheel. **Dundarroch**, 1922, on a promontory into Loch Ard, is a delightful neo-

McKean

Top: Duchray Castle.
Above: David Marshall Lodge.
Right: Dundarroch.
OPPOSITE: Inversnaid.

INVERSNAID

regency building with a classical porch, harled
with trelliswork. There are scant remains of
170 **Duke Murdoch's Castle**, early 15th century
occupying Dundochil islet on the far side.
Ledard, a handsome white harled, black
marginned, largely 19th century, farm complex,
was the location of the **Scotch Hairst Kirn** in
1821, immortalised in **Three Nights in
Perthshire**.

Loch Ard became the location for one or two
larger 19th century houses including **Mellmohr**,
1886, by Charles and Thomas Leadbetter, a
large Arts and Crafts building harled with red
sandstone dressings. **Corrienessan** built in
1887 by J. J. Burnet, in red stone with half
timbered gables and a verandah — displaying an
unusual fusion of American and Norman Shaw
influence.

Inversnaid

McKean

171 What remains of the **Barracks**, 1719, the same
vintage as those of Ruthven and Bernera, is now
incorporated into part of a farm steading.
Although erected as part of the general policy of

WILLIAM AND DOROTHY
WORDSWORTH passed through
Inversnaid on their first Scots trip.
The poet espied a nymph amidst
the bracken:
*Sweet Highland Girl, a very shower
Of beauty is thy earthly dower!
Twice seven consenting years have
shed
Their utmost bounty on thy head:
And these grey rocks; that household
lawn;
Those trees, a veil just half
withdrawn;
This fall of water that doth make
A murmer near the silent lake;
This little bay; a quiet road
That holds in shelter thy abode—
In truth together do ye seem
Like something fashioned in a dream;*

INVERSNAID also provided
Gerard Manley Hopkins with the
inspiration for one of his most
evocative poems:
*This darksome burn, horseback
brown,
His rollrock highroad roaring down,
In coop and in comb the fleece of his
foam
Flutes and low to the lake falls home.*

*A windpuff-bonnet of fáwn-fróth
Turns and twindles over the broth
Of a pool so pitchblack, féll-
frówning,
It rounds and rounds Despair to
drowning.*

*Degged with dew, dappled with dew
Are the groins of the braes that the
brook treads through,
Wiry heathpacks, flitches of fern,
And the beadbonny ash that sits over
the burn.*

*What would the world be, once bereft
Of wet and of wildness? Let them be
left,
O let them be left, wildness and wet;
Long live the weeds and the
wilderness yet.*

RCAHMS

RCAHMS

Top: Inversnaid Barracks.
Above: the Hotel.

controlling the Jacobite districts after the 1715 rebellion, the choice of remote, and poorly populated Inversnaid was almost certainly caused by the activities of Rob Roy MacGregor who had made this inhospitable shore of Loch Lomond his home after his eviction from his policies from Craigroyston further south. His men attacked the workmen during construction. Two substantial barrack blocks faced each other across a large courtyard, the flanks consisting of a wall-walk on top of vaulted cellars, at the corner of each of which was a projecting tower. Not very much remains to be seen — a number of walls, loopholes — picturesque desolation amidst piggeries.

172 **Inversnaid Hotel**, down on the spectacularly beautiful shore is much the sort of building one expects from a mid-Victorian hunting lodge: a large, spreading building, with lots of gables.

WALTER SCOTT passed that way in 1792, and found *a garrison consisting of a single veteran . . . the venerable warder was reaping his barley croft in all peace and tranquility; and when we asked admittance to repose ourselves, he told us we would find the key of The Fort under the door.* In 1820 it was occupied by two women who kept *a kind of an inn* in the ruins, but by 1828, Scott reported it *totally dismantled.*

122

Rob Roy MacGregor (1671-1734) was the youngest son of Donald MacGregor of Glengyle, from whom he inherited Inversnaid, although he also appears to have owned Craigroyston, near Rowardennan. In 1691, some 21 years before he became an outlaw, he was involved in a cattle-rustling enterprise at Kippen, which developed into an open battle between the villagers of Kippen and the MacGregors. The affair was subsequently known as the *herriship* (the harrying) of Kippen. In 1712, an associate of Rob Roy absconded with £1,000 which had been raised from various gentry — including the Duke of Montrose — for the purchase of cattle. Those who had subscribed — including Montrose — pursued Rob Roy for their money: his property at Craigroyston was forfeited, the stock and furniture arrested and sold in such circumstances that led Rob Roy to regard the Duke of Montrose as his enemy thereafter. He moved north to seek the protection of the Earl of Breadalbane in Glendochart, although he also sought the protection of John, second Duke of Argyll. Rob Roy figured in the 1715 rebellion, and, although hedging his bets notoriously at Sheriffmuir, was listed in the Act of Attainder for treason in 1717.

In November 1716 he carried out his most famous raid, here described by an angry Duke of Montrose: *Mr Graham, Younger of Killearn, being on Monday last in Monteith . . . collecting my rents, was about 9 o'clock that same night surprised by Rob Roy with a party of his men in arms who, having surrounded the house and secured the avenues, presented their guns in at the windows, whilst he himself entered the room with some others with cockt pistols, and siezed Killearn with all his money, books, papers and bonds and carried all away with him to the hills. . . .* Graham was held on an island on Loch Katrine for two or three days, before being restored to the Duke with all his papers, but less the money — to the extent of about £1,000 sterling.

Pursuit became hot, and in the next three years Rob Roy was captured three times, and each time managed to escape. In 1720, he settled in Balquhidder, and in 1725 General Wade arranged a formal pardon. In 1734 he died at Balquhidder.

THE MACGREGORS are widely credited with inventing the term blackmail — the levying of black meal by a protection racket. Witness the following agreement of 1658-9, which the Bailie of Duntreath, Archibald Edmonstone caused to be published at the church of Strathblane: *upon reading of ane petition given in be Captain MacGregor, mackand mention that several heritors and inhabitants of the Paroches of Campsie, Dennie, Baldernock, Strablane, Killearn, Gargunnock and others, within the shirrifdome of Stirling did agree with him to oversee and preseve their houses, goods and gear frae oppression, and accordinglie did pay him; and now that some persons delay to mac payment according to agreement and use of payment, thairfoir it is ordered that all heritors and inhabitants of the paroches affoirsaid, make payment to the said Captain MacGregor of their proportions for his said service, to the first February last past, without delay.*

The statue of Rob Roy below the town hall in Stirling, by Scotland's most distinguished modern sculpture Benno Schotz, is clearly based on the contemporary painting by an unknown artist, which emphasises his short stature and long arms. Graham of Gartmore described him *a person of sagacity, who neither wanted strategem nor address; and, having abandoned himself to all licentiousness, set himself at the head of all the loose, vagrant and desperate people of that clan in the west end of Perth and Stirlingshire, . . . on these accounts, there is no culture of ground, no improvement of pastures . . . in short no industry . . . here the laws have never been executed . . . in short, here is no order, no authority, no government.*

One of his escapes was celebrated in a ballad, the *Chieftain's Return: Roy Gregarach is come again Roy Gregarach is come again Craigroyston now shall be his ain For he's got free and back again.*

173 **The Homesteads** Mc▸
c. 1910, James Chalmers.
A pioneering group of detached and semi-detached houses and cottages with steeply pitched red pantiled roofs and white harled walls, some subsequently buttressed. The colony, which included its own farm and a smallholding with each property, derived from the combined momentum of the Independent Labour Party, the Scotland Branch of the Garden Cities Association, and the Scottish Guild of Handicraft. The concept was that of a self-sustaining agricultural co-operative, on land leased from the Crown. Among the artists and craftsmen who fashioned the fireplaces, furniture, tiles, handles, and letterboxes were Jessie King, Eliza Kerr, P. W. Davidson, H. T. Wyse, Hugh Allan and Janet Aitken. See **The Homesteads** (1984) by Aitken, Cunningham and McCutcheon.

Cambusbarron

An ancient village on the slope of the Touch hills, commanding a superb view, a centre for weaving and spinning since the 18th century. The Parkvale and Hayford Mills, on the valley floor, employed more than 1,000 people. **Hayford**, founded by the Smiths in 1860, is a square, three storey building in brilliantly patterned red and white brickwork, a tower and cupola in one corner.

The Main Street runs parallel with the hill, the vaguely Art Nouveau **Bruce Memorial Church**, 1910, by McLuckie and Walter dignifying the junction with the road to St Ninian's. According to tradition, Bruce took sacrament in the chapel on this site on the eve of Bannockburn (just before — or after — slaying

Top: Stirling from Cambusbarron. In the right foreground are the Parkvale and Hayford Mills. Just behind, to the right in the trees, are the Homesteads, the co-operative farm on the plain in the left. In the distance the crag of Stirling rock.
Above: The Homesteads.

de Bohun). The houses date mostly from the 18th and 19th centuries, some stone, some harled, close-packed together for protection. The two northernmost houses — **Ledie View** — and **Beech Villa** are grander, whilst one in Murray Place has an inset lintel dated 1762.

RCAHMS

74 **Gartur**
Early 19th century
A small, 18th century, classical lodge gate leads over the hill down to the regency mansion of Gartur, a grand classical frontage tacked on to a quite small 17th/18th century house at the rear. Two storey and basement of well-dressed ashlar, the facade is dominated by the projecting entrance bay with its fine pilastered fanlit doorway and ironwork balcony above.

175 **Touch House**
John Steinson, 1747.
In common with Airth and Gargunnock, Touch is of a fusion of an old tower and a fine house; in all three, one face is classical whilst the rear is almost entirely 16th/17th century; and in all three the contrast between the two heightens the interest and enjoyment of the building.
Its north face is very defensive — a raised mound protected by the junction of the Touch Burn and another, upon which stands a long, dormered and harled 17th century range, abutting a great, parapetted and crow-stepped stone keep.
The south facade is a three storey, classical composition with a projecting, pedimented and urned central bay, built by Gideon Gray from 1757. The pediment is wonderfully carved with the arms of the Setons of Touch. The architectural details are understated but excellent: pediments above the windows of the first floor, a rusticated ground floor (together indicating that the principal rooms are on the first floor). An elegant oval staircase with cast-

Left: Gartur House.
Below: Cambusbarron Main Street showing the Bruce Memorial Church.

RCAHMS

HBC

176

iron baluster leads to the three splendid first floor apartments which contain notable panelling, plasterwork by Thomas Clayton, and tapestries. If the staircase is original, it is one of the earliest uses of cast-iron balustrades in a staircase like this in Scotland. **Seton Lodge**, 18th century, enlarged later, is a white harled, two storey early Regency villa, whose centre three bays are bowed out to emphasise the central stone, fanlit Tuscan doorway.

Meiklewood
c. 1830.
Home of the Grahams of Meiklewood since 1615, the house is a grand, stone neo-Tudor design dominated by its gabled, projecting porch. Octagonal shafts rise to the roof, flanking a superbly shaped dormer gable. The interior was splendid in Tudor Gothic. The nearby stable courtyard with its gabled bellcotted entrance pend has considerable charm.

Gargunnock
An ancient village that more resembles a French community than Scots, clinging to a hillside, wholly overshadowed by the Gargunnock Hills towering behind, which, wrote Drysdale in 1904, *almost hide the sun from the villagers during the winter*, in compensation for which the setting provides a *view as extensive and beautiful as can be seen in almost any part of the world.*

Top: Touch House.
Above: Meiklewood.

OPPOSITE top: Gargunnock Village and the distant hills.
Upper middle: Gargunnock Church.
Lower middle: Gargunnock House.
Bottom: Watson House.

McKean

The heart of the village at what is called the Square, by the 18th century bridge over the Gargunnock burn. The **Parish Church**, 1626, was constructed as a plain, crowstepped rectangle, extended in 1604, bellcote added in 1702. At the east end there is a 1701 loft for the estates of Boquhan and Leckie. The first school, linked to the church, began in 1652. **Dunning House** (formerly the Manse) is a yellow harled, two storey, 18th century house. The picturesque houses around **The Square** are mostly 18th century as are most of the older houses up the Main Street; some harled, one or two in stone, many probably built for the weavers and shoemakers who lived here. Other local industries included sawmilling and oak-spale baskets. A strong tradition of dissent is recorded, and until the **Dissenters' Chapel** was built in 1843, Dissenters walked every Sunday to the Erskine Kirk in Stirling.

McKean

177 **Gargunnock House**
1580-1794.
An H-shaped house plan dominated by its three storey classical facade. An L-shaped tower house, now the heart of the house, was extended to the north east, complete with corbelled turret and, in the 17th century to the north west. In 1794, the pedimented and balustraded classical facade was created with the addition of a south east wing. Fine interior details.

RCAHMS

Leckie
Leckie, and the more gigantic Watson House (formerly New Leckie) are split by the Leckie Burn running down from the Gargunnock Hills.
178 **Watson House**, 1830, a Church of Scotland home, is very splendid stone Jacobean with tall shafted chimneys, elegant mouldings, crinkly parapets and gothic windows à la Gillespie Graham.

Sanderson

RCAHMS

BOQUAN WAS famous for adventurous husbandry, the proprietor — General John Fletcher-Campbell — founding the Gargunnock Farmers' Club in 1796. In 1845 it was said of the estate: *Less than a century ago, the lands lay almost entirely in a state of nature, unprofitable to the landlord and repulsive to the agricultural operators; bad roads, the want of enclosures, the stiffness of the soil and ignorance of that species of farming which was not suitable to the District. But headed by the proprietor of the estate of Boquhan and stimulated by his energetic and skilful examples all the heritors in the Carse of Stirling united or rather vied in effort such as draining, ditching, hedging, planting and other improving operations, and speedily achieved a complete and delightful change of both their aspects and their character. Toward the close of last century, only about two acres on the property of Boquhan remained in a mossy condition.*

THE SENSATION of independence created by Kippen's commanding site is reinforced by the story reported by the historian Buchanan of the time of James V. The first Buchanan owner of Arnprior demanded the purchase of part of the load of a carrier going to Stirling. On being told that the load was for the King, Buchanan replied, *Tell him if he is King of Scotland I am King of Kippen and need some of my Royal Brother's provisions.* The King, with retinue, duly paid a visit to Arnprior, interrupting Buchanan's meal with *The Gudeman of Ballochgeigh humbly requests an audience of the King of Kippen.* The meeting proved successful, with the King inviting His Royal Impertinence back to the Royal Palace of Stirling.

179 Leckie House
16th century
A recently restored T-shaped laird's house whose three storey, harled posterior and high chimneys may be glimpsed from the main road. The old entrance was under an arch, defended by a yett, into the stem of the T. Twin projecting circular turnpike stairs fill the corners between the stem and the main block. The principal rooms were on the first floor where a well-carved stone fireplace yet survives. This was the seat of David Moir, from 1688, remembered in Stirling from the Moir of Leckie's Ludging. On 13th September 1745, the Lady of Leckie entertained Bonny Prince Charlie, her husband being detained in Stirling Castle by the opposition.

180 Boquhan
A distinctive, turreted, L-shaped Edwardian gatehouse by Steele and Balfour leads to the policies of Boquhan, a white harled, green 181 painted 1959 mansion. **The Steading** of Boquhan 1817, is one of the best examples of a grand stable courtyard in the District, its principal feature the pedimented entrance pend, capped by a stone octagonal clock tower, itself completed by an attenuated onion-shaped, green copper dome.

182 Burnton of Boquhan, on the old road, c. 1798, are single storey cottages aggrandised by a projecting central bay in red ashlar, containing round-headed windows flanked by pilasters which support a pediment above.

183 Auldhall
An 18th century, two storey farmhouse with a projecting bowed stair, attached to an earlier L-shaped cottage, possibly on the site of vanished Boquhan Tower.

McKean

Kippen

Oot o' the world as they say, *and intae Kippen.*
The red sandstone tower of **Kippen Church**,
1823, by William Stirling, rises proud on its
hilltop to mark the effective end of Kincardine
Moss and the beginning of more rolling
countryside to the west.

84   **Kier Know of Drum**, a promontory
overlooking the Carse was the location of a
stockaded wooden building of the early Middle
Ages. Just to its west is a forlorn relic — the late

85 18th century **Laraben Doocot** — surprisingly
late, and built of brick. The northern slopes of
Kippen become more densely occupied toward
the top with picturesque houses and short rows
of cottages dug into the hillside to enjoy the
relative shelter and outstanding view. Many
probably date from the 18th century, and most
are white painted, some decorated with trellis
and other climbing plants; a vindication, if you
like, of the Kailyard view of Scots history. The
houses facing the road are grander, ones to
observe being **Tarfield**, a symmetrical three
bay, two storey house of 1797, and **Helensfield**,
distinguished by its vividly eccentric,
rectangular, ornamental fanlight above the door
(its shape and pattern making a mockery of the
origin of the term fanlight). The nub of Kippen
lies around the picturesque churchyard, and the
ruined, bellcoted west gable of the Old Kirk: the
neighbouring buildings have crow-stepped
gables, and a cobbled street leads down to the
Black Bull Inn, 1729, harled with red
sandstone margins. The **Smiddy**, nearby is also
18th century, and is maintained as a working
operation by the National Trust for Scotland.

McKean

Top: Kippen and the Church.
Above: the Old Kirk of Kippen
looking across the Carse of Forth
to the Highland hills.

Glebe House and the Cross Keys Hotel are both 18th century and the 1906 **Recreation Rooms** are white harled with red sandstone details including a venetian window. **Ben View** is high quality Victorian — dressed stone, twin barge boarded gables, and a flamboyantly bracketted doorpiece.

Cauldhame consists of a delightful, one-sided street (a burn being on the other). **Arnmoulin** is inter-war council with Dutch gables whilst **Springburn** is a smart 1970 harled and mono-pitch roofed cottage extension by Les McGeogh.

Baxter

White House

186 Gribloch House

1937-39, Basil Spence with Perry Duncan. Possibly the largest private house of the '30's in Scotland, built for the steel family Colvilles, Gribloch is set high in a streamlined park, with a superb view north to the Trossachs. A two storey white harled mansion with a flat parapet and invisible roof, the design has some 1930's characteristics — particularly the curved walls and portholes of the outbuildings. The main building, with its fountains and swimming pool, decorative plasterwork and oval hall with curving staircase is much more Hollywood Regency.

RCAHMS

187 Wrightpark
1750

Three storey, tall, stern, neo-Palladian country house hidden in trees on the old road. The front is of well-dressed stone, whilst the flanks and the rear are harled. The five bay principal facade consists of a rusticated ground floor, supporting the main rooms above, themselves dignified by giant Ionic pilasters. The composition is completed with a shapely piended roof, and twin central chimney stacks, architraved windows, and a fine three-bay pediment, punctuated by a bullseye and capped by urns.

Also on the old road is the newly restored 188 **Mains of Glinns**, a substantial, harled 17th century laird's house, with a fine 1743 doorway in the James Gibbs manner.

IN 1750 THE young widow of Wrightpark and heiress of Edinbellie, Jean Kay was abducted by Roy Roy's son, Robin Oig, and allegedly forced by him into marriage. After protestations by her family, the pair were separated as roughly as they had come together: the lady died, and the MacGregor was executed.
Rob Roy is frae the Hielands come
Down to the Lowland border
And he has stolen that lady away
To haud his house in order
(with her inheritance of course).

McKean

Left: Main Street Fintry, showing the millworkers' flatted houses on the left.
Below: Culcreuch Castle.

Fintry

The original village of Fintry, now called Clachan, is commemorated by the wet mock Gothic 1823 **Parish Church**, possibly by William Stirling who designed the much grander school by the Village Cross; a few pleasant cottages, and houses including crowstepped **Dunmore House**, 1723, the former manse.

Of the 15th century Castle of the Grahams of Fintry, half a mile upstream from the picturesque **Low Bridge of Gonachan** (1751), barely the foundations remain — indicating a long narrow block with a tower at one end and outbuildings. Further upstream overlooking Loch Carron are the surviving earthworks of the castle of John de Graham, and on the hillside just above the western end of Fintry is a well preserved motte and bailey.

All was changed by the purchaser of Culcreuch Castle, Peter Spiers, who came to Fintry from Renfrewshire in 1769 and, 20 years later, founded a cotton mill on the banks of the Endrick. *A very improving village,* thought Garnett in 1800, *an entire new town having been built for the acommodation of the manufacturers since the introduction of cotton manufacture. The houses are built according to a regular plan, each consisting of two storeys and garretts.* The houses on the south side of the main Fintry road were feued in 1794, roughly as they are now, with gardens across the road going down to the river. Like the later Colonies in Edinburgh, the front door opened only into the ground floor flats, the upper floors and attic being a separate flat reaching from external stairs at the rear. All that remains of the mills is the fine, four square stone **Mill House**, a symmetrical three-storey building, access to a hay loft in one gable.

Culcreuch Castle

15th century onwards.
A classical gate lodge whose centre bay projects with a fine porch leads uphill to the Castle

RCAHMS

which nestles in a hollow *embosomed in wood, a great part of which is fine old timber: not withstanding its bartizans and thick walls it is commodious, and yields to no other residence in the country for the venerableness of its appearance and the beauty of its situation.* Thus in 1841.

It is a splendid 15th/16th century keep, extended to the east and the north in the 18th century, virtually intact with its barrel-vaulted ground floor, the main hall on the first floor retaining an ogival-headed aumbry in one corner. The drawing room, in the 18th century wing, has good decoration and a classical fireplace.

194 **Edinbellie Church**
1742
A plain, barn-like T-shaped building (now altered for farm purposes) which was the first Secession Church to be built under the inspiration of the Reverend Ebenezer Erskine.

Ballikinrain Castle: original perspective by David Bryce.

RCAHMS

195 **Ballikinrain Castle**
David Bryce, 1868.
An unusually enthusiastic baronial mansion, for Sir Archibald Orr-Ewing, a Glasgow magnate. It is said that, in this building, the architect of such extravagances as Fettes College in Edinburgh had at last really gone over the top. Even its gateways — Victorian Gothic buildings encrusted with gargoyles, crow-stepping, carved stone and turrets — contribute to the overall magic.

Gutted by fire in 1913, allegedly caused by suffragettes protesting at Sir Charles Cayzer, it was restored in truncated from by C. H. Greig who fitted it out with material salvaged from Ralston House, Paisley, by David Hamilton and J. J. Stevenson.

Old Ballikinrain
17th century onwards.
On the one side, a plain early mansionhouse within an enclosed courtyard, with a well carved, architraved doorway and quoins, somewhat spoiled by a later roof. The other front presents a substantial early 19th century facade that has gables bowed out on either end, a pedimented centrepiece with roundel and heavy windows.

Boquhan Old House
1784.
A large, plain two-storey harled Georgian house, stone margins' dormer windows, consoled doorpiece and a square-headed fanlight.

RCAHMS

Above: Old Ballikinrain — the 17th century facade with later roof. **Left:** the main street of the "new village" of Balfron.

Balfron
The Clachan at one time was the chief, if not the only, point of attraction, wrote the Minister in 1841. *It still deserves pre-eminence, for here, the parish church still stands, surrounded by the burial yard, always an object of deep interest to the population. Here also is the smithy — and the old oak tree in which were fixed the jougs of the parish. But alas, the glories of the Clachan have passed away. It is now shorn of its importance by its immediate neighbour the new village of Balfron,* which sprung into existence with the introduction of manufacturers about 60 years ago. The **Parish Church** by John Herbertson of Glasgow, 1832, is distinguished by its square tower above the entrance. **Clachan House**, 1766, is a two storey, grey-harled building with a central doorway. **Orchardfield House** is a larger, oblong, cream-harled house with a fine internal curved stone staircase, with a mahogany handrail. The **Old Manse**, 1789, is a symmetrical Georgian house with extension, difficult to reconcile with the minister's 1841 statement that it was *originally poorly built and ill-finished, the heritors having in consequence been frequently called upon to repair it at considerable expense.*

ABOUT 1789, THE proprietors of Ballikinrain brought in the Buchanans of Carston (those responsible for Deanston) to build the Ballindalloch cotton works. But by 1841 working conditions had become harsh: *the wages are apparently low: and are certainly much lower than are paid for the same quantity of work done in Glasgow . . . they toil at what is termed long hours, and long enough these are, being from 6 am or even earlier to 8 pm and even later; and yet they are only able to earn a miserable pittance . . . The population has increased since 1792 but not so, we fear, in comfort nor in happiness in an equal ratio. On the contrary, there is in it very much misery arising from poverty and destitution; and if some new impetus be not given, by some means or other, in a few more years far away our children will have left the land.*

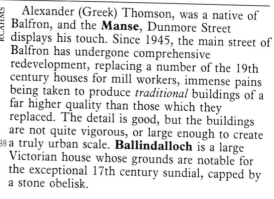

Alexander (Greek) Thomson, was a native of Balfron, and the **Manse**, Dunmore Street displays his touch. Since 1945, the main street of Balfron has undergone comprehensive redevelopment, replacing a number of the 19th century houses for mill workers, immense pains being taken to produce *traditional* buildings of a far higher quality than those which they replaced. The detail is good, but the buildings are not quite vigorous, or large enough to create a truly urban scale. **Ballindalloch** is a large Victorian house whose grounds are notable for the exceptional 17th century sundial, capped by a stone obelisk.

198

199 **Carbeth House**
17th/19th century
An old Scots house transformed into a *showy castellated mansion* about 1840, a porch and porte-cochere added in 1879.

200 **Little Carbeth**, Drumtian Road
Boys Jarvis, 1978.
U-plan, white rough cast building which combines traditional features — colour, pitched tiled roof, setting in the landscape, with smooth modern details and facilities. Staircase at the heel (also traditional) to link the two wings of the house: principal reception rooms at first floor level.

Killearn
The village wrote the minister in 1841, *is scattered and irregular; yet, as the generality of the inhabitants possesses fixed property, they are free from the vices and vicissitudes of a manufacturing population . . . the character of the parishioners is decent and pious occasioned mainly by the constant intercourse subsisting between householders and their domestics.* The centre of the village is the **Old Church**, the ruins of an elegant structure of 1734 on a much older site. Built of reddish sandstone, its distinctive features are its round-

Top: Balfron Manse, an early building by Alexander (Greek) Thompson.
Middle: Carbeth House.
Above: Ballindalloch Sundial.
Right: Little Carbeth.

McKean

headed windows with keystones, its quoins, and the raised margins of its doors and windows. The new **parish church**, now the church hall, 1826, is not unnecessarily ugly, but the **Parish Church**, 1880, by John Bryce is a handsome, vigorous, pointed Gothic design. The *comfortable and substantial* **Manse** dates from 1825, its stables and kitchen wing both considerably older.

The survival of many of the older houses at the centre of the village can be attributed to the activities of the Killearn Trust, founded in 1932 for the promotion and advancement of the welfare and interest of the inhabitants of the parish of Killearn. Trust buildings may be recognised by white paint, heavy black-painted margins, and red doors. In 1933, the Trust acquired and renovated three cottages in the neighbourhood of the **Black Bull Hotel.** The **White Horse Inn**, in the upper part of the village, is a good example of a small inn of the late 18th century, and the Toll House opposite is a single storey rectangular red sandstone building. The new **Health Centre** is well-scaled but vigorously modern behind which is an elegant modern house by John Laird. The **Buchanan Monument,** a grey ashlar obelisk designed by James Craig in 1788 to honour the celebrated Scots historian George Buchanan, dominates the village.

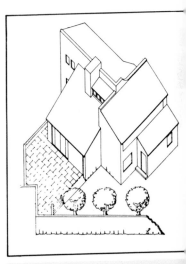

201 **Auchinibert**, 1906, was designed by Charles Rennie Mackintosh. The client's forceful English wife caused Mackintosh to deviate from Scots toward a Cotswold manor, with English Jacobean interiors. The strain of apostasy clearly proving too great for Mackintosh, the Shands brought Alexander Hislop in to finish the job.

202 **Killearn House**, 1816 is an elegant classical house. **Carston**, 1766, is a typical two-storey substantial Georgian farmhouse, with three bays,
203 its symmetry spoiled by a new bathroom window.

RCAHMS

DUNTREATH

GEORGE BUCHANAN (1506-82), was the son of a small Stirlingshire landowner, educated at Killearn parish school, St Andrews University, and in Paris under John Major. The greatest latinist of his day at a time when latin was in universal use as a scholarly tongue, he was in many ways the epitome of the cosmopolitan Renaissance man, first in the Court of Queen Mary, and then attaining the influential post of Tutor to James VI over whom, as a boy, he exercised a compelling influence. Though the King never shared Buchanan's severe Genevan Calvinism, his pedagogue imbued him with a respect for learning and a distinctive latin accent. *All the world knows* he said in a speech to Edinburgh University after the Union of the Crowns, *that my master George Buchanan was a great master in that faculty. I follow his pronunciation both of his Latin and Greek, and am sorry that my people of England do not the like; for certainly their pronunciation utterly fails the grace of these two learned languages.* Buchanan was the author of *De Jure Regni Apud Scotes* a constitutional work (some of whose features appear in the American Constitution) which stated, inter-alia, that the King was not above the Law. His contemporary, Sir James Melville said this of him: *Mr George was a stoick Philosopher who looked not far before him. A man of notable endowments . . . much honoured in other countries, pleasant in conversation . . . also religious but was easily abused and so facile that he was led by every company that he haunted . . . he was naturally popular and extremely revengeful against any man who offended him*

204 **Moss**
1808

Replaced the original thatched-roofed, oak-beamed house in which George Buchanan was born in 1506, a chair and table being created out of the old beams in his memory. This plain harled square house with protruberant porch was extended by Charles Rennie Mackintosh for Sir Archibald Laurie, his wing mansarded: it is now demolished although some of his fitments survive.

205 **Glengoyne Malt Distillery**
1836

Picturesque courtyard of mainly white-painted buildings.

RCAHMS

206 **Duntreath Castle**
14th century onwards.

Duntreath, Ballewan and neighbouring parts all once formed part of the great earldom of Lennox. Judging from old prints, the castle consisted of a walled courtyard dominated by the powerful 14th century keep and lined with pleasant, 16th century crow-stepped ranges. The unique gatehouse stands apart, probably as the only survivor of an outer wall. In the 18th century, the Edmonstones removed to Ireland, leaving the castle to ruin. They returned in the 1860's, carried out some alterations, and — in 1890 — commissioned Sydney Mitchell and Wilson to reconstruct. Mitchell responded to this, one of his biggest commissions, with a combination of vandalism and flair. All save the keep and gatehouse was demolished or altered — part of the picturesque 1863 alteration surviving in the interior of the courtyard. Mitchell added superstructure to that, and a wholly new garden front of beautifully cut stone with dormer windows, a round tower, and projecting bay. The building has been since reduced, leaving the keep (which still retains its original roof structure) free-standing.

Duntreath Castle in mid-Victorian times.
Left: Carbeth Guthrie.
Below: Levern Towers.

07 Ha'Ballewan
1702

A small, crowstepped, near-symmetrical, two storey house with a moulded doorpiece. An original panelled room surviving within.

10 Carbeth Guthrie, 1817

A plain, square, painted whinstone mansion, with piended roof and projecting, semi-circular Doric porch, built by a West Indian plantation owner, John Guthrie who made significant changes to the landownership pattern of the area, diverting roads, selling off parts of his land and buying other estates so as to create a major estate. According to the Duke of Montrose, Guthrie had *found it little better than a peat hagg, and left it the **diamond of the desert**.* The house was extended by John Baird in 1855.

THE BLANE VALLEY

There are a number of late Victorian/Edwardian houses in the Blane Valley, Strathblane and
09 Blanefield. They include **Craigallian**, 1885, a large house with a neo-mediaeval tower designed by James Ritchie for A. G. Barns Graham on the site of a 17th century laird's house. **Dunmullin** is gabled and barge-boarded, with a very pretty lodge, whilst **Levern Towers**, 1938, is a swash-
13 buckling V-plan house with towers and turrets, built for himself by John Lawrence.

RCAHMS

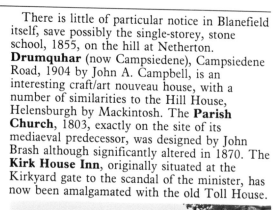

McKean

There is little of particular notice in Blanefield itself, save possibly the single-storey, stone school, 1855, on the hill at Netherton. **Drumquhar** (now Campsiedene), Campsiedene Road, 1904 by John A. Campbell, is an interesting craft/art nouveau house, with a number of similarities to the Hill House, Helensburgh by Mackintosh. The **Parish Church**, 1803, exactly on the site of its mediaeval predecessor, was designed by John Brash although significantly altered in 1870. The **Kirk House Inn**, originally situated at the Kirkyard gate to the scandal of the minister, has now been amalgamated with the old Toll House.

Holmes

214 **Leddriegreen House**, an exquisite example of a Georgian laird's house, consists of a plain two-storey block with quoins, flanked by single storey pavilions with blind venetian windows 215 and pediments. **Ballagan House**, circa 1760, and gloriously Victorianised in 1896 with Italianate tower, replaced the tower of the Earls of Lennox across the river, beneath the Spout of Ballagan, a 70 foot waterfall.

Some older buildings representing the former village of **Edenkill** survive in Drumbrock Avenue, at the corner of which is a pleasant late 18th century house. **No 8**, 17th century, is the former Edenkill House, complete with crow-stepped gables, later extended when it became the home of drovers. **No 6** is contemporary. The road to Mugdock, formerly Edenkill Road, passes by interesting large houses: **no 40**, 1957, by Horace Hamilton, is an elegant single-storey U-planned bungalow; whereas **Deil's Craig** is a grand neo-Scots Edwardian mansion turreted and crow-stepped.

216 **Deil's Craig Dam**, 1957, by Jack Holmes is an elegant modern pavilion on a sloping rocky site, its white geometrics making a handsome contrast with its wild setting.

Hamilton

Craigend Stables
1812, Alexander Ramsay.
If the stables of vanished Craigend are so fine —
gothic windows, mullions, hood moulds, turrets
and a crenellated parapet, what have we lost
with the demolition of the Smith's Mansion? It
had fallen on hard times, being used as a zoo
prior to its abandonment. **Smith's Folly** was
erected part as an ornament, and part as a
viewpoint.

Mugdock
The sometime prominence of Mugdock is
commemorated by what was once known as the
three towns of Mugdock, of which **Eastertown**
is a large Victorian mansion, **Middletown** an
earlier Georgian farmhouse; and **Westerton** the
actual borough itself which consists of some
pleasant cottages and houses and stupendous
baronial stables. The extraordinary view south to
Glasgow confirms its strategic location: by
holding Mugdock, the Grahams of Montrose
held the main communication between Glasgow
and the north.

HBC

OPPOSITE top: Strathblane Church.
Middle left: Deil's Craig Dam.
Bottom left: 40 Edenkill Road.
Main column: Leddriegreen House.

Above: Smith's Folly, Craigend.
Left: Mugdock Castle.

McKean

Mugdock Castle
From 14th Century
Set on a fortified plateau once surrounded by the
loch on three sides, the castle was originally
built as a courtyard, with towers in at least three
of the corners. One of these, dating from the late

Above: Mugdock Castle in the late Victorian period showing the baronial house by James Sellars, with the tower behind. The walled garden and the loch are clearly visible, as are the ruins of the Chapel on the right.

14th century, survives almost to its original height, and another its later vaulted basement only. A large window, in the curtain wall between, implies that the Hall might have been at this point. From the south front projected a rare portcullis gateway, of which the portcullis chase still survives in well-cut stonework.

The tower is entered at the first floor up an external staircase, which used to link with a wall walk. Its ground storey is rib-vaulted with a fine fireplace, and the staircase to the upper storey of the tower is within the thickness of the wall. The quality of the carved stonework, and the unusual nature of this plan — (since the towers do not project from the main curtain wall, but are enclosed within it) makes Mugdock unique in Scotland; more of a fortified manor house than a castle.

In the late 15th century the promontory was enclosed by a large curtain wall with early gunloops, against which were built stables and other offices, with external staircases to the first floor. The remains of the chapel, thirled to a latrine tower survive to the north.

The Castle was **herried** by the Buchanans in the Civil War, but repossessed by the Montrose family soon afterwards, who built a new mansion within the castle walls facing south over the loch, with a fine series of stepped walled gardens down to the loch, much of which survives with the Ducal monogram. This 17th century block incorporated a third tower within it, but was otherwise a plain two storey with attic building with carved dormer windows. The castle was abandoned by the Montrose family in favour of Buchanan at the end of the 17th century. In 1883 J. Guthrie Smith appointed James Sellars to rebuild the east block into an L-shaped baronial mansion linked to the old tower by a half timbered arched, first floor walkway. At the request of his client, Sellars incorporated into the new building a number of the details, dormer windows and carved panels of the old house. After the Second World War and the ravages of the Ministry of Defence it remained empty, although shortlisted as a possible site for the Burrell Collection. The Castle and the estate were the subject of a number of different development ideas, eventually to be presented by Sir Hugh Fraser to Central Regional Council, who are now repairing what remains of the buildings and converting them into a country park (architects Boys Jarvis). There was a time when a local expression of incredulity was *Mugdock Castle's no a pyot's nest yet.* It has been so this last 20 years.

Arnprior

19 Small village on a bluff overlooking the Lake of Menteith. **Arnprior Farm** 18th century, is a substantial two storeyed building at the front, and three at the back, its quality emphasised by a fine central doorway with a fanlight. The cottage on the edge of the road down to the Lake of Menteith has crow-stepped gables and pantiles.

RCAHMS

20 **Garden**

Above: Garden.

1824, William Stirling.
Modest but stately classical mansion house with a Greek Doric columned porch, cream harled with sandstone dressings. Incorporating an earlier 1749 house at the back, it is very much in the model of the houses David Hamilton and Peter Nicholson built for the Glasgow mercantile gentry.

BUCHLYVIE

Baron of Buchlyvie
May the foul fiend drive ye,
And a' to pieces rive ye
For building sic a town
Where there's neither horse meat
Nor man's meat
Nor a chair to sit down

Buchlyvie

Hillside village consisting mainly of a single wide street flanking the A811. **The Church**, 1835, is a belfried gothic cruciform church in red sandstone with wide-mouthed windows. **Old Spittalton**, nearby, 1738, is of the grander sort, two-storey, white harled with painted margins. The earlier **North Church**, 1751, is a long, low, plain single storey building whose round-headed windows and doors emphasised by their projecting margins and prominent keys. The **Village Hall** at the west end is dominated by a fine stone tower, with ball-finials and ogee-shaped roof. The houses in the village are generally of the 18th and 19th centuries.

Top: Buchlyvie Main Street.
Above: the 1835 Church, Old Spittalton on the left.
Right: Gartinstarry with a view across the Carse of Forth.

221 **Gartinstarry**, a mile to the north west, 1789, is a substantial white farm house with painted margins, skewputts, flanked by two single-storey wings gable to the road.

222 **Peel of Gartfarren**

13th century?
One of the best preserved homestead moats in Scotland, situated on the western edge of Flanders Moss; one of a small number in this area. The enclosure consists of a large irregular area enclosed by a bank and a ditch. It could represent the shape and general size of the now obliterated, and much more celebrated, Peel of Gargunnock some miles to the east.

223 Old Auchentroig

1702

In the country of the blind, the one eyed man is King. On the edge of the Highland Line, beyond which the majority of houses were single storey crofts built of stone and clay with turf for roofs, the diminutive two storey, harled stone mansion of Auchentroig must have seemed a palace: particularly with the addition of the simple architectural embellishments of crow-stepped gables, the moulded main entrance, and the heraldic panel above. The house retains its original double-thickness door and is very complete and unaltered: too unaltered in fact to be lived in. Its condition has been a matter of concern.

224 Balfunning House

Late 19th century — James Thomson of Baird and Thomson

Florid red stone baronial mansion on a bluff looking south. Notable circular tower with balustrade. Delightful old-Scots lodge gate.

Above: Old Auchentroig.
Left: Drymen.

Drymen

The parish of Drymen, like that of Aberfoyle, was entirely owned by the Duke of Montrose, and its prosperity was undoubtedly conditioned by the removal of the Duke from Mugdock to Buchanan, at the very gates of the village, in the early 18th century. The other cause of its expansion was the village's location on the post-1745 military road from Stirling to Dumbarton. It has now been bypassed, allowing it to settle back into its growing role as a tourist honeypot. That role is emphasised by the fact that its southern entrance is flanked by two major golf clubs, and that the two most notable buildings in the village are hotels — the celebrated **Buchanan Arms**, which is probably a mid-Victorian expansion of a large lodge, and the **Winnock**, which is the conversion of a row of late 18th century cottages lining one side of the village green, heavily extended but in sympathetic style on the south. The Drymen Pottery is equally celebrated.

The finest building is the **Parish Church**, 1771, a dramatic cream-harled T-shaped building with pink-painted quoins and margins, and a bellcote. There is an interesting upper gallery inside. The ancient site contains a number of old gravestones, including one to the occupier of Easter Balfunning, dated 1682. A number of unusual modern buildings have been attracted to the outlying areas, including an elegant, flat-roofed, single storey bungalow by John Laird, 1957.

226 **Dalnair**
1682

A large 17th century house with a single storey wing, with a projecting main entrance, with dates above topped by a crow-stepped gable. The house was probably built as a manse. **Dalnair House**, c. 1885, is a Glasgow merchant's house of the grander sort, with a striking parapeted tower rising above the trees at the entrance to Croftamie.

227 **Millfaid, Croftamie**
Boys Jarvis, 1980.

L-shaped, white roughcast building, slated roof, variegated roof line and modern details: making a virtue of inconspicuousness.

225 **Catter House**
1767

Catter survives virtually unaltered as a good example of the smaller Georgian country house: oblong on plan, two storeys high over a full basement, the walls harled with dressed cornice, quoins and margins. A central pediment rises above the cornice with a heraldic panel dated 1767. The chimney-stacks have scrolled cable-

RCAHMS

Left: Catter House.
Below left: Buchanan Castle.
Below: High Mains Farmhouse,
possibly by William Playfair.

moulded ornament. The main entrance is through a pedimented doorway approach up a curved two-way stair.

Sanderson

229 **Buchanan Castle**
The largest of the interesting remains in the Buchanan Estate, is the well-kept ruin of the Castle by William Burn, 1854. The main block, two-storeyed and dormered attic, terminating in towers at either end, is dominated by a three-storey spikily turreted entrance tower. The single storey classical **Lodge**, square in plan with a pyramid roof is an early 19th century confection by William Playfair, as may be the circular **Ice House**. The **Stables** form a two-storey courtyard with pedimented entrance. **The**
230 **Old House** (now the club house) is the remains of the house of 1724 which may itself have included parts of its predecessor. In 1725 William Adam produced an unrealised design for a grand and beautiful mansion for the Duke of Montrose, his son John worked there in the 1750's and James Playfair altered it in 1789.
231 **High Mains**, possibly designed by William Playfair, is a substantial symmetrical, white farmhouse with oversailing roof and a central

Sanderson

Below: Milton Church.
Right: Milton Farm.

232 pedimented porch. The **Smithy** on the main road to Balmaha, consists of an early 19th century *ferntoun* row with a smithy in the middle.

233 **Craigievern**
18th century
Up on the hills towards Garadhban Forest a three storey T-shaped Laird's house with stone margins emphasising its windows, and a grandly moulded, off-centre, main door.

Boys

Milton
236 **Milton Farm**, 18th/19th century, is a great bull of a building: powerful, sturdy-shouldered, muscular white walls and a pedimented ashlar porch for a snout on its front, and flank. The 235 attractive **Parish Church**, 1774, replaced that of Inchcailleach, an island on Loch Lomond from whose title — (the island of the Old Women) — one infers to have been the site of a nunnery. It is thought that old Buchanan House was placed on an axis so that the original church on Inchcailleach could be seen from it; of which all that remains is an excessively romantic graveyard and a number of individual stones.

234 **Gartincaber** is a pleasant 19th century house with mullioned windows and flanking single storey wings. The old Manse is an enlarged 1795 two storey, harled building.

Balmaha
The **Old Manse**, 1910, is a pleasant harled building with unusually shaped wings.
237 **Strathcashel Point** to the north contains the remains of an ancient enclosure, once thought to be a castle but more likely to have been a dark age religious enclosure; and a **crannog** lies just offshore.

RCAHMS

146

Inversnaid by Gerard Manley Hopkins is taken from the 1967 edition of the *Poems* edited by W. H. Gardner and N. M. Mackenzie (Oxford University Press).

WORKS CONSULTED FOR THIS GUIDE

The method of this guide precludes the normal system of reference for sources. The following works have, however, been used as primary reference sources: *Stirlingshire*, Volumes 1 and 2 RCHAMS, *New Statistical Account*, Stirlingshire and Perthshire, *The Beauties of Scotland*, 1805: Forsyth, *Gazetteer of Scotland:* 1845, *Landmarks of Old Stirling:* Ronald, *Old Faces, Places, Stories of Stirling:* Drysdale, *The Waverley Novels*, 1829 edition: Sir Walter Scott, *History of Scotland:* George Buchanan, *Nimmo's Stirlingshire; The Industrial Archaeology of Scotland:* John Hume, *The Third Statistical Account; Memoirs of Sir James Melvil of Halhill, Circuit Journeys:* Lord Cockburn, *Early Travellers in Scotland:* P. Hume-Brown, *Across the Tweed:* Theodore Fontane, *The Eye is Delighted:* Maurice Lindsay, *The Baronial and Ecclesiastical Architecture of Scotland:* R. W. Billings, *Scotland Illustrated, Journey from Edinburgh:* Alexander Campbell, *Tour Through the Highlands:* Garnett, *Royal Progress in Scotland:* Sir Thomas Dick Lauder, *Tour in Scotland:* Thomas Pennant, *The Old Country Houses of the Old Glasgow Gentry, The Parish of Strathblane:* J. Guthrie Smith. Sir Walter Scott's *Journal*, and extracts from *Letterbooks; Letters:* John Ramsay of Ochtertyre, *History of Scotland:* Lindsay of Pitscottie, *Three Nights in Perthshire:* Percy Yorke; *King's Park*, and *The Homesteads*, by Aitken, Cunninghame and McCutcheon.

In addition, there were numbers of guide books, leaflets, and books of anecdotes for Stirling, Dunblane, Callander, Aberfoyle, Killin.

ACKNOWLEDGEMENTS

The compilation of a book of this type is a team effort. Many people have contributed to either the information carried therein, to its accuracy, or to the illustrations. Of necessity, those about to be credited form only the foremost amongst those who have helped: David Walker, Adam Swan, John Gifford, Archie Ferguson (President of the Stirling Society of Architects), Alan Wightman (Chairman of the Stirling Civic Trust), Professor Erskine Wright, Dr Robert McIntyre, Robert Burnett, Alastair Brown, Mrs Jo Turnbull, R. McCutcheon, Allan Jeffrey of Stirling District Libraries, members of the Architecture, Planning, Surveying and Administration Departments of Stirling District Council, John Boys, Mrs Shiela Lyle, Ian Gow and the staff at the Royal Commission on the Ancient and Historical Monuments of Scotland, the Scottish Record Office, the Scottish Development Department, Erick Davidson, Robert Naismith of Sir Frank Mears and Partners, Sandy Smith, Gerry Crossan, Fiona Sinclair, John Norrie, R. McEachern, John Dunbar, Dr Frank Walker, John Yellowlees, Charles Strang, Mr Mitchell, Assistant Director of Planning, Stirling District Council, Professor Alistair Rowan, the National Gallery of Scotland, Ingval Maxwell, G. R. Barbour, Sotheby's, Geoffrey Stell, M. Pettigrew, John Knight and C. Sanderson. Particular thanks is due to Alison Kane for typing the manuscripts.

Front Cover Photograph: Chris Page, Development Department, Stirling District Council.

Production: Dorothy Steedman, Will Richardson, Charles McKean.

Photographic Credits: Each photograph is credited with its source alongside the photograph. The Publishers would like to thank particularly the Royal Commission on the Ancient and Historical Monuments of Scotland who, as before, have provided us with almost unlimited help. Thanks also goes to the Ancient Monuments Division of the Scottish Development Department, Adam Swan, The Historic Buildings Council, John Boys, the Library of the Edinburgh Architectural Association, the Property Services Agency, the RIAS Library, the author Charles McKean, the Scottish Record Office, the National Galleries of Scotland, Campbell Sanderson, Property Group of Stirling District Council, White House photography, Neil Baxter, and the architectural practices who submitted photographs of their buildings.

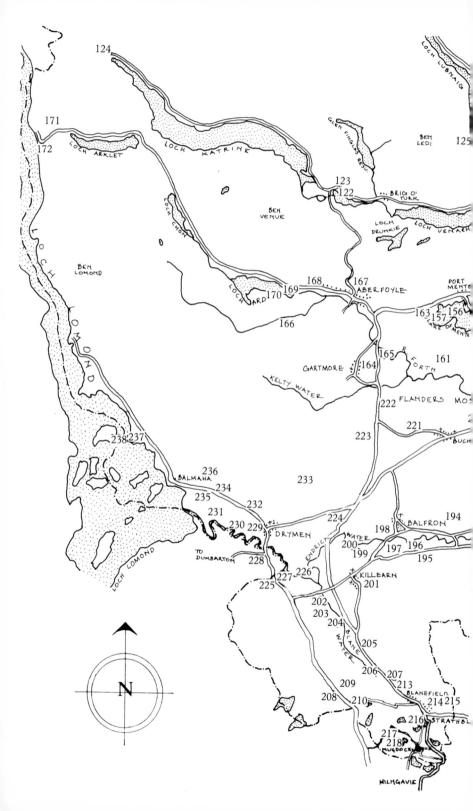

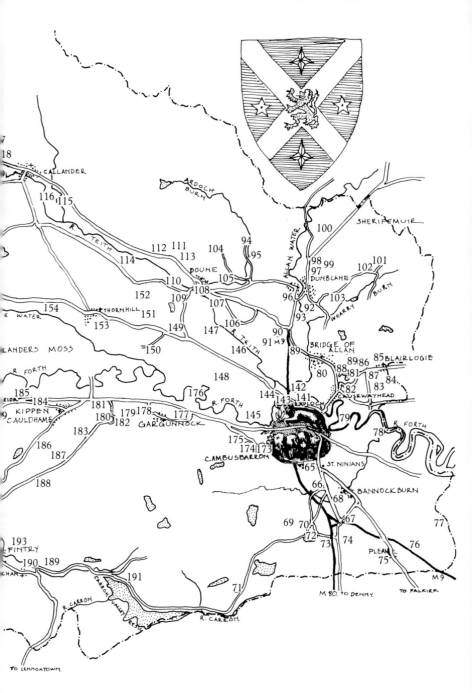

THE DISTRICT

INDEX